Tell Me
Everything

First published in 2005 by Bounty Books,
a division of Octopus Publishing Group Ltd.

Material previously appeared in:
Tell Me About (Bounty Books)
Tell Me Why (Bounty Books)
Tell Me When (Bounty Books)
Tell Me What (Bounty Books)
Tell Me How (Bounty Books)
Tell Me Where (Bounty Books)

This edition published in 2014 by Bounty Books,
a division of Octopus Publishing Group Ltd.,
Endeavour House,
189 Shaftesbury Avenue,
London WC2H 8JY
www.octopusbooks.co.uk

An Hachette UK Company
www.hachette.co.uk

Copyright © Octopus Publishing Group Ltd., 2005, 2014

ISBN: 978-0-753728-01-7

A CIP catalogue record for this book is available from
the British Library

Printed and bound in China

Tell Me Everything

Bounty Books

THE WORLD 8

The Animal Kingdom 9

The Plant World 33

Earth & Space 59

Prehistory 89

THE HUMAN BODY 114

Bones & Muscles 115

Heart & Circulation 133

Brain & Nervous System 147

Genetics & Reproduction 165

HISTORY 180

Who 181

How 195

What 213

When 229

Where 245

SCIENCE & TECHNOLOGY 260

The Earth 261

The Natural World 277

Discoveries & Inventions 289

The Solar System 303

INTRODUCTION

Whether you're looking up information for a project or coursework, or just out of interest, *Tell Me Everything* has the answers! Here is a taster of what you will find in more than 300 information-packed pages and fascinating fact files on related subjects.

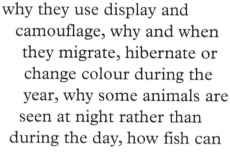

THE WORLD explores the planet we live on and the animals and plants with which we share it. Within this section, 'The Animal Kingdom' looks at how animals feed, why they use display and camouflage, why and when they migrate, hibernate or change colour during the year, why some animals are seen at night rather than during the day, how fish can breathe under the water and many other fascinating subjects. In 'The Plant World' subjects include how trees breathe, why leaves come in all shapes and sizes and how plants reproduce. In 'Earth & Space' we look at our planet itself: the shape of the ocean floor, how the continents were in different places millions of years ago, what glaciers and ice sheets are, what causes erosion, extreme weather, the effects that we are having on our planet, the atmosphere, the age of the Earth and the size of the universe. 'Prehistory' covers the development of life on Earth, fossils, the evolution and behaviour of dinosaurs, whether the dinosaurs were wiped out by an asteroid and how they were replaced by mammals.

In THE HUMAN BODY we look at the marvellous structure that we take for granted. In 'Bones & Muscles' subjects covered include what our skeleton does and how it works with the muscles to support us and allow us to move around, how bones

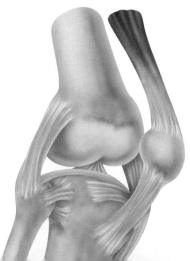

and wounds heal, the structure of joints and what happens to muscles during exercise. 'Heart & Circulation' explores the vital role these play in our lives, how the heart pumps, what valves are, what blood is made of and what blood groups are. 'Brain & Nervous System' shows how messages are flashed to and from our brains, how we feel and how instructions are passed from the brain, the brain's structure, how memory works, why we feel hungry, why we dream and even why some people are left-handed. 'Genetics & Reproduction' looks at the nature of chromosomes, how our genes dictate what we look like and how babies develop.

The HISTORY section explores all aspects of recorded human history, from great leaders and empires, to inventors and inventions, daily life, warfare and great civilizations. 'Who...' looks at famous historical characters, such as Alfred the Great and Boadicea, as well as great peoples from the past, including the Franks and the Hittites. 'How...' explores historical events on a deeper level, asking such questions as 'How successful were the Viking attacks?' and 'How did the United Nations begin?'. 'What...' covers significant historical events, for example, the Cuban Missile Crisis, the Battle of Britain and the signing of Magna Carta, as well as artifacts such as hieroglyphs and Stephenson's Rocket, and movements like Communism and women's suffrage. 'When...' takes a look at important events in world history such as the abolition of the slave trade, the first explosion of an atomic bomb and the opium wars, and examines ancient developments including the first use of honey, the first houses and the stone age. 'Where...' explores events and places from around the world, including the locations of Persepolis and the Silk Road and the Forbidden and Imperial Cities, as well as the expansion of the Muslim Empire, and where the

Romans bathed and held gladiatorial games.

SCIENCE & TECHNOLOGY explores geology, weather, life on Earth,

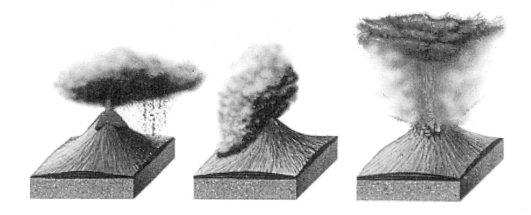

human technological achievements, the Solar System and deep space. 'The Earth' looks at how our planet moves around the Sun, earthquakes and plate tectonics, droughts, lightning, gravity and the structure of the Earth. 'The Natural World' examines how scientists like Darwin and Linnaeus learned about evolution and the classification of animals and plants, as well as about extinction, the colonization of the land by early plants, and answers fascinating questions such as 'When did Plants First Appear?' and 'How do water-dwelling insects breathe?'. 'Discoveries & Inventions' looks at inventions throughout history, from paper to planes and gunpowder to glass. 'The Solar System' explores the Moon, planets and other smaller bodies, such as comets, that travel around our Sun, and discovers the nature of stars, the Milky Way, black holes, galaxies and supernovas.

The World

The Animal Kingdom

WHY DO MOSQUITO BITES ITCH? 10
WHY DO MOTHS EAT WOOL? 11

CAN ANIMALS UNDERSTAND ONE ANOTHER? 12
WHY DO PEACOCKS HAVE SUCH BEAUTIFUL TAILS? 13

WHAT IS A VAMPIRE BAT? 14
DOES A COW REALLY HAVE FOUR STOMACHS? 15

WHAT IS THE LARGEST ANIMAL IN THE WORLD? 16
WHERE WOULD YOU FIND A COBRA? 17

WHERE DO RHINOCEROSES LIVE? 18
WHAT IS A MUTE SWAN? 19

HOW DOES A KINGFISHER CATCH ITS FOOD? 20
WHAT MAKES A MOLEHILL? 21

WHERE DOES A CRICKET PRODUCE ITS SONG? 22
IS IT TRUE MALE SEAHORSES BECOME MOTHERS? 23

WHAT IS AN AMPHIBIAN? 24
HOW DO FROG EGGS HATCH? 25

HOW DO BIRDS FLY? 26
HOW FAST CAN BIRDS FLY? 27

HOW MANY KINDS OF FISH ARE THERE? 28
HOW CAN FISH BREATHE UNDERWATER? 29

HOW DO BIRDS KNOW WHEN TO MIGRATE? 30
HOW FAR DO BIRDS MIGRATE? 31

WHEN WILL WHALES BECOME EXTINCT? 32

WHY DO MOSQUITO BITES ITCH?

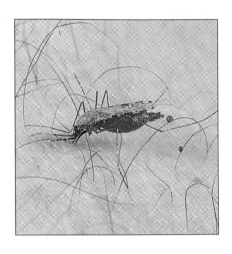

The itchy welt that forms on the skin when a person has been 'bitten' by a mosquito is, in fact, an allergic reaction to the insect's saliva, which it injects into the skin in order to prevent its victim's blood clotting. A mosquito cannot actually bite because its jaws do not open, but the middle of its proboscis has six needlelike parts, called stylets. These are protected by the insect's flexible lower lip, or labium, most of the time. When a mosquito 'bites', the lip slides out of the way like a sleeve as the stylets puncture the skin. The channels made by the stylets allow saliva to flow into the wound, thus allowing the insect to sip blood more easily. Only female mosquitoes bite and only those of a few of the 3,000 or more species attack animals and people.

FACT FILE

Some of the worst diseases that people and animals suffer are spread by mosquitoes. Some species are carriers of such serious infections as Dengue fever, yellow fever, malaria and filariasis.

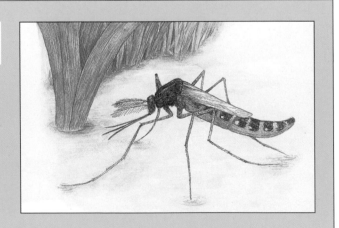

WHY DO MOTHS EAT WOOL?

Eyed hawk moth

Most people think that small moths, called 'clothes moths', make the moth holes in our clothes by chewing them. There are various species, including the webbing moth, the casemaking moth and the tapestry or carpet moth. It isn't the adult moths that cause the problem, because they don't eat, but the caterpillars that do the damage. The female moth lays her eggs on wool, or sometimes other fabrics, and after between 4 and 21 days, depending on the species, they hatch into tiny caterpillars. The casemaking moth caterpillar turns the wool it eats into a case, which it lines with silk and drags around with it. There it lives as a caterpillar until it turns into a pupa, and eventually emerges as an adult.

FACT FILE

When at rest, eyed hawk moths resemble a dead leaf. If alarmed, they open their forewings to reveal striking eye markings on the hind wings. This is likely to scare predators such as birds.

Death's head hawk moth

Poplar hawk moth

CAN ANIMALS UNDERSTAND ONE ANOTHER?

Howler monkeys

FACT FILE

Otters live in habitats where it's easier to use sound to communicate with each other rather than visual signals. As well as a warning growl, they have a repertoire of various chirps, chuckles, screams and squeals to express their feelings.

Although animals cannot actually talk to one another, they have means of communicating by using visual and noise signals. Just as we use expressions, sounds and gestures to indicate how we are feeling, many animals make noises and signs. Mute swans, particularly males, will raise their wings, swim towards an intruder and hiss to warn him off, and other birds sing both to attract mates and defend territory. Howler monkeys do actually howl to defend their territory, and this acts as a warning as it carries through the forested areas of Venezuela. Animals can also communicate by using smell, and many mammals mark their territories with scent.

WHY DO PEACOCKS HAVE SUCH BEAUTIFUL TAILS?

We often hear the expression 'proud as a peacock' or 'vain as a peacock,' and that is because the peacock seems to take great pleasure in displaying its beautiful feathers. The display is done solely by the male to attract a female bird. The female, the peahen, does not have these beautiful feathers. The most obvious thing about the male peacock is the trail of greenish feathers with bold eyespots, which aren't tail feathers, but grow from his back. The male also has a shiny metallic greenish-blue breast and neck, greenish feathers on his back that lead to the train and dark purplish-blue underparts. During courtship, the male bird spreads his train into a gorgeous fan as he parades in front of the female. He practically goes through a dance as he tries to convince the peahen that he is very handsome.

FACT FILE

Indian peafowl, the correct name for this species of peacock, originate from India and Sri Lanka, where they can be seen roaming in the wild.

WHAT IS A VAMPIRE BAT?

Whiskered

Geoffrey's   **Natterer's**   **Bechstein's**

Several different bats in Central and tropical America are called vampire bats. At night, they bite warm-blooded animals such as cattle, horses and birds with their razor-sharp front teeth and drink their blood. Their saliva contains an anti-coagulant that prevents the victim's blood clotting. They do not, in fact, suck blood, but lap like cats. They are named after the fictitious monsters, such as Count Dracula, that suck blood from people, but although they have been known to attack sleeping humans, it is not common. One of the smallest of them is the common vampire bat, which is about 3 inches (8 cm) long and has reddish-brown fur on its body.

FACT FILE

Many species of bats live in colonies that may have thousands or even millions of members. Others live alone or in small groups. Most bats spend the day sleeping in their roost.

Long-eared bat

DOES A COW REALLY HAVE FOUR STOMACHS?

FACT FILE

Cows, sheep and goats have no front teeth in the upper jaw. Instead, the gums form a tough pad.

The simple answer to this question is no – cattle have only one stomach with four compartments, called the *rumen*, the *reticulum*, the *omasum* and the *abomasum*. This complex system enables them to bring partly digested, softened food back into their mouth to be re-chewed and then re-swallowed; this process is known as chewing the cud. Animals with these four-part stomachs are called *ruminants*. Micro-organisms in the digestive system allow the animals to break down the food to obtain as many nutrients as possible. In the fourth cavity, the 'true' stomach, gastric juices mix with the food, which then passes to the intestine for absorbtion.

WHAT IS THE LARGEST ANIMAL IN THE WORLD?

FACT FILE

The largest land mammal is the African elephant which can weigh up to 6.9 tons (7 tonnes).

The blue whale is the largest animal that ever lived on Earth. It is also the loudest animal on Earth. These enormous mammals eat tiny organisms, like plankton and krill, which they sift through baleen (a horny substance attached to the upper jaw). They live in pods (small groups). These grey-blue whales have 2 blowholes and a 2–14 inch (5–30 cm) thick layer of blubber. Blue whales are rorqual whales, whales that have pleated throat grooves that allow their throat to expand during the huge intake of water during filter feeding. Blue whales have 50–70 throat grooves that run from the throat to mid-body.

Blue whales

WHERE WOULD YOU FIND A COBRA?

Cobras can be found throughout the Philippines, Southern Asia and Africa and are well known for their intimidating conduct and deadly bite. Cobras are recognized by the hoods that they flare when angry or disturbed; the hoods are created by the elongated ribs that extend the loose skin of the neck behind the cobras' heads.

The king cobra is the world's longest venomous snake. It averages 12 ft (3.7 m) in length but has been known to grow to 18 ft (5.5 m). It has olive or brown skin, with bronze eyes. The king cobra is found in the Philippines, Malaysia, southern China, Myanmar (formerly known as Burma), India, Thailand and the Malay Peninsula.

The venom of cobras often contains a powerful neurotoxin and acts on the nervous system. Venoms have some medicinal uses – for example, some are used as painkillers in cases of arthritis or cancer.

FACT FILE

The spotted salamander is one of the larger members of the mole salamander family reaching nearly 8 inches (20 cm) or more. They lay up to 200 eggs in a single mass in early spring, usually after the first warm rain.

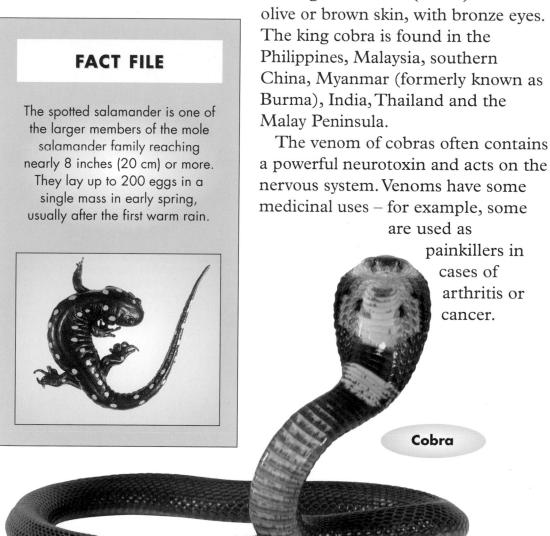

Cobra

WHERE DO RHINOCEROSES LIVE?

Rhinoceroses are found in two regions of the world: Africa and Asia. The black rhinoceros and white rhinoceros live in Africa, while the Indian, Javan and Sumatran rhinos live in parts of Asia. Black, white and Sumatran rhinos have two horns, while the Indian and Javan species have only one. The horns are made of densely packed, coarse hair, and are used only in defence or in fights between males.

Rhinoceroses are vegetarians and have to eat vast amounts of grass and other plants every day to maintain their huge bodies and usually move about very slowly to avoid wasting energy. They are distantly related to horses, but instead of hooves, have three toes on each foot.

FACT FILE

Rhinoceroses are usually placid, but if they feel threatened, they will charge. Despite their stubby legs, they can run remarkably fast – at speeds of up to 38 mph (48 kmh).

WHAT IS A MUTE SWAN?

FACT FILE

Swans nest along the shores of rivers, waterways and the coast in the summer and move to large lakes in the winter. Mute swans feed mainly on underwater plants, but also graze on marshland during the winter.

Swans are waterfowl that are closely related to, and larger than, ducks and geese. The mute swan has an orange bill with a prominent black knob and swims with its neck held in a graceful S-shape. They aren't, in fact, mute, and make snorting noises and hiss when threatened. When they are flying, their wings make a throbbing sound with each wingbeat.

In summer, breeding pairs are territorial and the males can be very aggressive in defence of their nest and cygnets, but in winter they may feed in large flocks. They feed by upending and reaching down with their long necks to nibble underwater plants.

HOW DOES A KINGFISHER CATCH ITS FOOD?

Kingfishers are birds with large heads, heavy, pointed bills and stubby legs and tails. Some are brightly coloured like the common kingfisher, while others, for example the laughing kookaburra, are camouflaged.

A kingfisher may sit for hours on a branch beside water looking for fish near the surface. Then, after perhaps hovering for a moment in midair, the bird dives after a fish, either seizing it in or spearing it on its bill. It bobs back to the surface and uses the membranes between its middle and outer toes to launch itself back into the air. Back at its perch, it tosses the fish into the air and swallows it headfirst. Other sources of food that kingfishers exploit include crustaceans, frogs and insects.

FACT FILE

Kingfishers burrow in the walls of river banks or sandbanks, or between the roots of upturned trees. They dig a tunnel a good 3 ft (1 m) long with a hollow at the end where the eggs are laid on a nest of fish bones.

WHAT MAKES A MOLEHILL?

Molehills are small conical mounds of soft earth, often connected by slightly raised lines of earth. These are made by moles. Each mound lies above one underground room of a mole's complicated home and the raised lines are above the passages between individual rooms or runs where it is digging for food.

A mole is a small mammal with a stocky, well-muscled body. With its large, strong forelegs and wedge-shaped head, it is perfectly adapted for its life burrowing through soil. The mole is a fast, tireless digger, and its

front paws have long, broad nails and turn outward, which makes them ideal for shovelling earth. Moles don't need to see and they are almost blind, with tiny eyes, but they have excellent hearing, which enables them to locate their prey, such as earthworms and subterranean insects.

FACT FILE

The central chamber of a mole's home is larger than the other rooms and contains a nest of leaves and grasses. Moles are born naked, but they start to grow fur at the age of two weeks. They leave the nest after five weeks.

WHERE DOES A CRICKET PRODUCE ITS SONG?

Crickets are jumping insects that are related to grasshoppers, and species include the European house cricket and the common cricket of the United States. They live in fields, meadows and in the grass alongside roads. Most songs are produced by the males, although females of some species do also sing. Unlike grasshoppers, which produce sounds using their legs, crickets do so by rubbing their front wings together. They don't have ears, but hear using organs in their front legs. Cricket songs are mating calls that are designed to attract females and usually consist of a series of chirps or a set of trills.

Cricket

Crickets differ from grasshoppers in several ways other than how they produce sound. Most crickets have wings that lie flat over each other on their backs, while those of grasshoppers are slightly raised, and most cricket antennae are longer than their bodies, unlike the short ones that grasshoppers possess. There are also wingless crickets and some that have only very small wings. Crickets eat plants and small insects.

Grasshopper

FACT FILE

A grasshopper is an insect that can leap about 20 times as far as the length of its body. If a human being had that same leaping ability, he or she could jump about 120 ft (37 m).

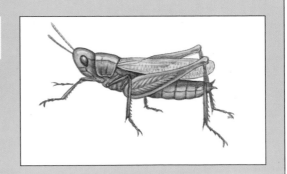

IS IT TRUE MALE SEAHORSES BECOME MOTHERS?

The seahorse is a small fish and acquired its name because its face looks horse-like. We are used to the idea that it is always the female that bear the offspring, but in seahorses it is the reverse. The female seahorse, when she lays her eggs, puts them into the broad pouch beneath the tail of the male. When the young have hatched and are ready to leave the pouch, the mouth of the pouch opens wide. The male alternately bends and straightens his body in convulsive jerks and finally a baby seahorse is shot out. After each birth the male rests, and when all the babies are born he shows signs of extreme exhaustion, including going very pale in colour.

FACT FILE

The seahorse has been described as having the head of a horse, the tail of a monkey, the pouch of a kangaroo, the hard outer skeleton of an insect and the independently moving eyes of a chameleon.

WHAT IS AN AMPHIBIAN?

The internal organs of an amphibian

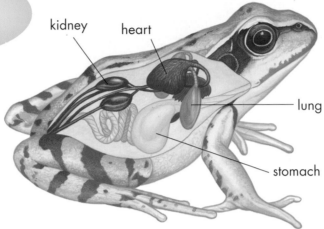

kidney

heart

lung

stomach

FACT FILE

Some brightly coloured amphibians produce poison in glands on their skin. The bright colours warn birds and animals not to eat them. The poisons are among the most powerful known to humans. In South America, poison from the poison arrow frog is added to the arrow tips used by the Indians for hunting.

From an evolutionary point of view, amphibians are halfway between fish and reptiles. There are 4,400 living species of amphibian, including frogs, toads, newts and salamanders. Many live mainly on land, but most spend at least some of their lives in water.

Frogs and salamanders are able to breathe through their damp skins to a certain extent, both in the water and on land, but toads must rely largely on their lungs and cannot remain in water for long. Toads and frogs are similar in many ways, although toads usually have rougher, drier skins and may waddle rather than hop as frogs do. Some toad spawn is produced in strings, like necklaces, rather than the mass of eggs laid by a frog. The largest amphibian, the Chinese giant salamander, is 6 ft (1.8m) long.

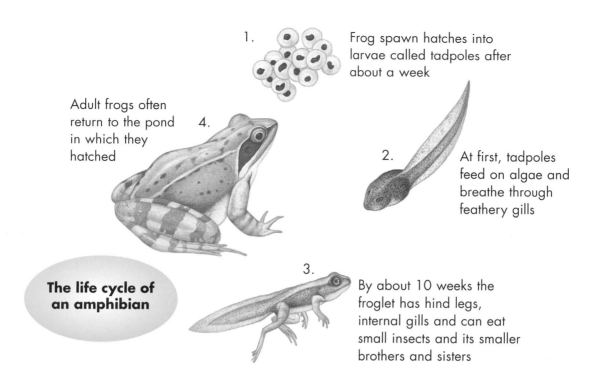

1. Frog spawn hatches into larvae called tadpoles after about a week

Adult frogs often return to the pond in which they hatched

4.

2. At first, tadpoles feed on algae and breathe through feathery gills

The life cycle of an amphibian

3. By about 10 weeks the froglet has hind legs, internal gills and can eat small insects and its smaller brothers and sisters

HOW DO FROG EGGS HATCH?

Most amphibians lay their eggs in water. Frogs' eggs are called spawn. They are protected from predators by a thick layer of jelly. Inside this a tadpole develops. When it hatches out, it is able to swim, using its long tail, and breathes through gills. As a tadpole grows, first hind legs and then fore legs begin to grow. Lungs develop, and the young frog is able to begin to breathe with its head above water. Gradually the tail shortens until the young frog resembles its adult parents.

FACT FILE

The tree frog lives in the rain forests of South America and uses the pools of water in the centre of certain tropical plants. Although it can swim, it spends much of its life out of water, among the leaves of trees where there are plenty of insects for food. It has sticky toes that enable it to climb.

HOW DO BIRDS FLY?

The bodies of birds are specially modified to give them the power of flight. Their bones are hollow to keep them light. Their bodies are also extremely lightweight, allowing them to glide and fly with the minimum of effort. For example, an eagle has a wing span of more than 7 ft (2 m) and yet it weighs less than 10 lb (4 kg). Birds also have air sacs linked to their lungs to give them extra oxygen as they flap their wings.

However, flying is not just a matter of flapping wings up and down. It is a mixture of gliding and powered flight. When the wings are flapped they move in a complicated way, scooping air downwards and backwards. The wing actually twists so that the air is pushed back in the right direction to give lift. The wings are twisted again on the forward stroke so that they slide easily through the air without slowing down the bird's flight. A bird's feathers, which help to reduce wind resistance in flight, are ideal because they are very light, yet also strong and flexible.

FACT FILE

The falcon is a bird of prey which feeds on other birds and small animals. It is equipped with powerful talons and a sharp beak in order to kill and dismember its prey. When the falcon dives on its prey it closes its enormous wings and drops like a stone to pick up speed. Powerful muscles in the bird's legs help to cushion the huge impact of the strike.

The internal organs of a bird

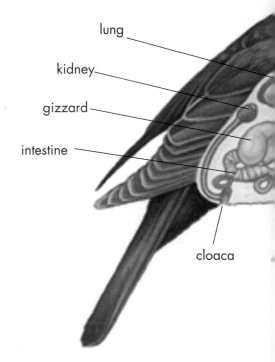

lung

kidney

gizzard

intestine

cloaca

HOW FAST CAN BIRDS FLY?

The first question is: 'How do we measure how fast they fly?' They don't fly in straight lines and their speed will be greater if the wind is behind them or if they are diving. Figures have been published for some species, but not all experts agree with them.

In general, the heavier a bird is, the faster it needs to fly to stay in the air. One expert believes that the fastest recorded flight for a bird was that of a homing pigeon going at 94.2 mph (150.72 kmh).

A few speeds, however, are generally agreed. Some species of ducks and geese can go about 63 mph (100 kmh). Peregrine falcons can fly at up to 75 mph (120 kmh), while hummingbirds reach speeds of 56 to 60 mph (90 to 95 kmh). Starlings are thought to fly at about 45 to 50 mph (70 to 80 kmh). Swifts can achieve almost 60 mph (95 kmh) and swallows usually about 25 mph (40 kmh), which helps them to make their long migration flights quickly.

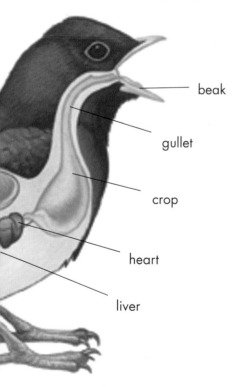

beak

gullet

crop

heart

liver

FACT FILE

Some birds cannot fly at all. Such birds include penguins, who use their wings in water, enabling them to swim very fast. The penguin shown below is a rare yellow-eyed species. There are only about 3,000 of them left in the world.

HOW MANY KINDS OF FISH ARE THERE?

Fish have existed for millions of years and have evolved into thousands of different types. There were fish in the oceans before the dinosaurs walked on the land. There are around 40,000 different kinds of fish and they exploit every conceivable watery habitat on the planet.

Fish are divided into three general types: cartilaginous, bony and lungfish. The cartilaginous fish, whose skeleton is made of flexible cartilage rather than rigid bone, include sharks, skate and rays. Bony fish, as their name suggests, have a bony skeleton and are covered with scales of a similar substance. Members of this group of fish are the most common and account for over 90 percent of all fish. Lungfish are a special type of fish because they have two sets of breathing equipment, possessing both gills and lungs. This type includes mud skippers.

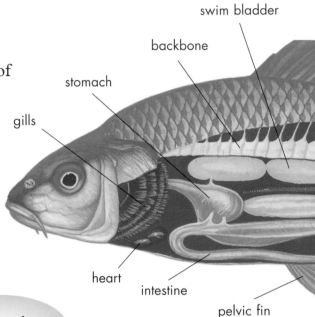

swim bladder

backbone

stomach

gills

heart

intestine

pelvic fin

Cross-section of a fish

FACT FILE

Salmon breed in small freshwater streams but spend most of their life in rivers and seas. To breed, they return to the stream where they hatched. They even leap up waterfalls in order to reach their spawning grounds.

HOW CAN FISH BREATHE UNDERWATER?

Fish are able to breath underwater because they have special organs called gills. Gills are bars of tissue at the side of the fish's head. They have masses of finger-like projections that contain tiny blood vessels. Water goes into the fish's mouth and flows over its gills. The gill filaments take in oxygen (which is dissolved) from the water and pass it from there into the fish's blood. In this way the gills have the same function as the lungs of air-breathing animals. If water is contaminated, fish need to take oxygen from another source. Some attempt to come to the surface of the water and take in oxygen from the air. However, their gills are neither suitable nor adept at processing oxygen from the air.

Fish are able to smell, although they do not use their gills for this. They have two small nostrils on their heads which act as organs of smell. The sense of smell is much more developed in some fish than it is in others. Sharks, for example, use their keen sense of smell to hunt down and catch other animals to feed on.

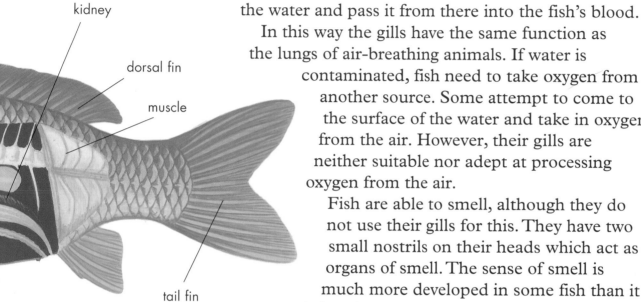

kidney

dorsal fin

muscle

tail fin

FACT FILE

Piranhas are very aggressive fish and can be dangerous in large numbers. Piranhas are supposed to be able to strip all the flesh from a pig or cow in a few minutes, but they are probably not dangerous to humans unless attracted to blood.

FACT FILE

Caribou usually live in relatively small numbers. However, when the time comes for them to migrate in search of food, they form herds of up to 3,000.

HOW DO BIRDS KNOW WHEN TO MIGRATE?

People have always been fascinated by why particular birds are present in summer but not in winter, and vice versa, even though they didn't understand it. Even just a few hundred years ago, some people thought that swallows hibernated under ponds during the winter. Even now, we still don't have all the answers.

What is migration? In this sense it is the movement of birds south from their summer breeding grounds to their winter feeding grounds in autumn and the return north in spring. Other forms of migration are moving from inland to the coast or between high and low ground.

Some go to warmer regions because they couldn't survive the cold. Others have to leave because their normal food is unavailable and they would starve if they stayed. But how do they actually know when to make this long flight? It is believed that birds can tell when the days get shorter (and longer in spring) and this acts as an 'alarm clock' to tell them that it is time to move along. Some birds, such as migrating swans or geese, seem to take the weather into account as well and stay at stopping-off points longer if conditions are suitable rather than move on.

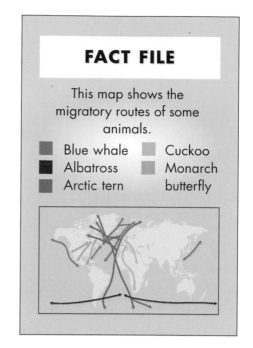

FACT FILE

This map shows the migratory routes of some animals.

- Blue whale
- Albatross
- Arctic tern
- Cuckoo
- Monarch butterfly

HOW FAR DO BIRDS MIGRATE?

Now we know why birds migrate, the next question is how far do they actually fly to find better conditions.

The champions among birds that migrate are the arctic terns. These amazing birds will travel as much as 22,000 miles (35,000 km) during the course of a year, going back and forth. It nests over a wide range from the Arctic Circle to as far south as Massachusetts. It will take this bird about 20 weeks to make its trip down to the antarctic region and it averages about 1,000 miles (1,600 km) a week.

Most land birds only make short journeys during their migrations. But there is one bird, the American golden plover, that makes a long non-stop flight over the open ocean. It may fly from Nova Scotia directly to South America, a distance of about 2,400 miles (3,800 km), without stopping.

We are not certain that birds start and end their migrations on the same day each year. But there is one bird that comes pretty close to it. It is said that the famous swallows of Capistrano, California, are thought to leave on October 23 and return on March 19, but of course their date of departure and arrival has been found to vary from year to year.

WHEN WILL WHALES BECOME EXTINCT?

Archaeological evidence suggests that primitive whaling, by Inuit and others in the North Atlantic and North Pacific, was practised by 3000 BC, and it has continued in remote cultures to the present. All whale species are becoming less common due to the fact that they have been regularly hunted for food and oil. Other factors are environmental pollution and drift net fishing. The grey whale was hunted almost to extinction by 1925 but was placed under complete international protection and since the 1940s has increased in numbers. Some of the larger species of whales can be seen in Europe as they pass by during migration.

FACT FILE

The humpback whale was also hunted almost to extinction, and its numbers dropped from 100,000 to 3,000 today. It is now generally protected.

The Plant World

WHAT ARE SUCCULENTS? 34
WHAT IS DODDER? 35

CAN PLANTS FEEL? 36
WHY IS HOLLY ASSOCIATED WITH CHRISTMAS? 37

WHAT ARE CHANTERELLES? 38
WHICH IS THE LARGEST KNOWN FUNGUS? 39

WHICH PLANT IS USED TO THATCH A ROOF? 40
WHAT IS THE FRUIT OF THE OAK? 41

WHY DO PLANTS NEED ROOTS? 42
WHICH PLANTS HAVE NO TRUE ROOTS? 43

HOW DO LEAF SHAPES VARY? 44
WHERE DID THE FIRST WILD STRAWBERRY GROW? 45

WHAT IS MADE FROM THE WILLOW TREE? 46
WHAT IS BARK? 47

WHAT IS PEAT? 48
WHY DOES A PINE TREE HAVE CONES? 49

WHAT ARE STOMATA? 50
WHICH IS THE BIGGEST FLOWER OF ALL? 51

HOW DO TREES GROW? 52
HOW DO LEAVES GROW? 53

HOW DO FLOWERS DEVELOP THEIR SCENT? 54
WHAT HAPPENS IN FLOWERS? 55

WHY DO PINE TREES STAY GREEN ALL YEAR? 56
WHAT ARE PERENNIAL PLANTS? 57

WHAT IS POISON IVY? 58

WHAT ARE SUCCULENTS?

Cacti

FACT FILE

Cacti have many rare and beautiful features, developed during a long and slow evolutionary process. One of their principal characteristics is the ability to adapt to harsh conditions, which would cause most other plant groups to perish quickly.

Succulents are plants that have organs such as leaves, stems or roots that are capable of storing water in order to survive extended periods of drought. All the plants in the cactus family are considered stem succulents. During periods of moisture, the stem swells and then during droughts slowly contracts. Cacti that have ribs are particularly well adapted to this as the ribs fill in and contract like an accordion. Cacti get their name from the Greek word *kaktos* meaning thistle.

WHAT IS DODDER?

Dodder is a strange, totally parasitic plant. When its tiny seeds start to grow, they put up thin threads that begin to twist in ever-increasing circles. Most seedlings die, because they fail to find the right sort of plant to take their food from. But if one seed finds the right host, it quickly attaches itself and pushes absorbing organs into the plant. The root of the seed then withers and dies, since the dodder plant now takes all of its food from the host. The most popular host plants are alfalfa, clover and flax. Dodder has tiny pink leaves that have no need for chlorophyll, which enables most plants to make food from sunlight. In late summer, dodder produces small, pink flowers and then masses of tiny seeds.

FACT FILE

Once dodder has established itself, it produces a mass of pink threads which cover the host plant and weaken it severely.

CAN PLANTS FEEL?

Although plants do not have feelings in the same way that we do, they can certainly respond to different stimuli. They are able to grow towards a light source, even if turned upside down. Some plants have very sensitive leaves, which will fold up if touched. Others have leaves that open and close according to the time of day. The Venus flytrap has sensitive leaf tips. When an insect lands on tiny hairs on the leaf, the pairs of leaves snap shut, trapping the insect inside. Plants are even able to perspire. Although you can't see this happening, if you were to place a plant inside a plastic bag and fasten it, after a while you would see drops of

FACT FILE

Some plants have sensitive hairs on their leaves. If an unsuspecting insect lands on these sticky hairs, in no time at all it finds its legs hopelessly entangled.

water form on the inside of the bag. The moisture you can see comes from the leaves of the plant.

Lords and ladies

WHY IS HOLLY ASSOCIATED WITH CHRISTMAS?

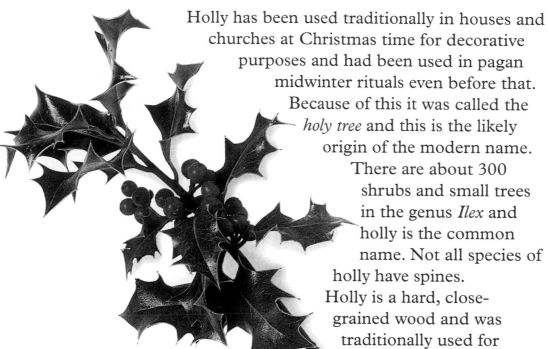

Holly has been used traditionally in houses and churches at Christmas time for decorative purposes and had been used in pagan midwinter rituals even before that. Because of this it was called the *holy tree* and this is the likely origin of the modern name. There are about 300 shrubs and small trees in the genus *Ilex* and holly is the common name. Not all species of holly have spines. Holly is a hard, close-grained wood and was traditionally used for musical instruments.

American and English hollies are evergreen trees that have glossy green leaves and red berries that make colourful Christmas wreaths. However, the berries (which are actually drupes, i.e. fruits with stones) are poisonous to humans.

FACT FILE

The poinsettia is a popular houseplant also used as a Christmas decoration. What look like the bright red petals are actually a kind of leaf. The real flowers are the tiny green dots in the middle.

WHAT ARE CHANTERELLES?

Chanterelles are mushroom-like fungi with funnel-shaped caps. The delicious and fragrant golden chanterelle is a delicacy prized by gourmets. Chanterelles are characterized by the form of their spore-producing surface, which is smooth and veined.

Mushrooms are important to our environment as they help keep soil fertile for the growth of plants. As mushrooms grow, they break down the dead material that they feed on, such as old leaves, and release nutrients back into the soil that the plants can use again in future.

Many insects and small mammals eat mushrooms as they are an important source of nutrients in themselves.

Golden chanterelle

Trumpet chanterelle

FACT FILE

The term tooth-fungi covers a range of unrelated species which all have spines or teeth on which spores are produced. Because of pollution, many of these are becoming rare.

WHICH IS THE LARGEST KNOWN FUNGUS?

The giant puffball is the largest known fungi. It can grow as large as 4½ ft (150 cm), although an average fruit body is the size of a football. Just one fruit body will produce about 7,000,000,000,000 spores. The puffballs are ball-shaped fungi, and are any shade of white to tan. They range in size from smaller than a golfball to larger than a basketball. When a puffball matures, its spores become dry and powdery. If touched, the puffball breaks open and the spores escape in a smoke-like puff.

Black Bovista

Scaly Meadow Puffball

FACT FILE

Flies and other insects are attracted to the stinking, slimy spore mass of the common stinkhorn. When they fly off after feeding, they carry away spores stuck on to their bodies. This is the way in which the stinkhorn spreads to new locations.

WHICH PLANT IS USED TO THATCH A ROOF?

The material normally used to make roofing thatch is common reeds, which are tall grass-like plants. They grow in almost all temperate and warm regions. They are found in a variety of habitats, from low upland meadows to wet lowlands and shallow lakes and ponds. Reed marsh is a valuable wildlife habitat if managed properly. The reeds are usually cut in the autumn, arranged into dense bundles and laid in layers on roofs. The thatch is waterproof and provides good heat insulation for the house. If laid and maintained correctly, a thatched roof should last for up to 40 years. Traditionally, the bundles are held in position with pegs made from strips of willow, although chicken wire is commonly used now to help keep the reed in place.

Common reed

FACT FILE

In many wetland areas, reeds spread rapidly, crowding out other types of marsh grass. For this reason it has to be regularly cut down. Reed grass has been used in the production of paper.

WHAT IS THE FRUIT OF THE OAK?

Oaks mature slowly and will not usually flower until they have reached 20. But they live a long time and many oaks live between two and four centuries. The fruit of the oak tree is called the acorn and is an ovoid nut in a small cup. In spring, oaks produce small, yellowish-green flowers. Copious amounts of windborne pollen are produced by the male catkins. The fertilized female flower will become an acorn that will start off green and go brown by the autumn. Depending on the exact species, acorns range from under $1/2$ inch (13 mm) to more than 2 inches (51 mm).

FACT FILE

The Oak Leaf Roller Moth lays small groups of eggs on oak twigs. In spring, the caterpillar feeds on oak leaves, which they roll up with silk.

WHY DO PLANTS NEED ROOTS?

Roots are not pretty and bright like leaves and flowers, but plants could not do without them. Anchored in the soil, they hold plants upright against wind and weather. They also grow out and down in search of water and minerals, which are drawn all the way up to the leaves. Because trees grow to such

enormous heights, the roots need to grow outwards to balance the spread of the branches above. Most roots grow in the top 1 ft (30 cm) of soil. This part contains most of the minerals the tree needs to survive. Every single root grows a mass of tiny hairs near its tip to enable it to absorb water from the soil. There are little pockets of air in the soil. Without these, roots would simply wither and die.

FACT FILE

There is one plant that does survive without any roots at all, and that is called Spanish moss. It grows in subtropical climates where the air is very wet. It absorbs all the moisture it needs through its fine, thread-like leaves.

WHICH PLANTS HAVE NO TRUE ROOTS?

Liverwort

Liverworts, hornworts and mosses do not have true roots. They are anchored to the ground by hair-like structures called rhizoids that resemble roots. A liverwort absorbs water over its entire surface and dries out quickly, so most grow in damp, shady environments.

Moss has a short stem which grows from the rhizoids. It is covered by tiny leaves in a spiral pattern. The leaves contain chlorophyll, a green substance the plant uses to make food. In many cases, a vein runs the length of the leaf from the stem to the tip. This vein, called the costa or midrib, strengthens the leaf and transports food and water. Many mosses grow in moist or aquatic environments. However, certain mosses can survive extremely dry conditions. Their need for water changes with the amount of water available in the environment.

Other plants that do not have roots include lichens and air plants. The latter cling to larger plants and absorb nutrients from rainwater.

FACT FILE

Lichens have no roots. They have an outer layer of fungal cells that are pigmented green, brown or yellow. This protective layer, called the upper cortex, covers a zone of green or blue-green algal cells.

Moss

HOW DO LEAF SHAPES VARY?

Pinnate

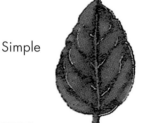

Palmate

Pinnate, with pinnately lobed leaflets

Simple

Palmately lobed

FACT FILE

Some plants have all their leaves in a ring at the base of the stem. This is known as a rosette.

The shapes of plant leaves vary considerably. The edges of leaves may be smooth or jagged. The leaf blades may be undivided (simple), or they may be divided (lobed) in various ways. Some leaves may be made up of separate leaflets. The commonest types of leaf shape are shown above.

The leaves themselves may be arranged on the plant in different ways, and this is usually standard for any given type of plant. A leaf arrangement which has single leaves at each level is called alternate. Leaves arranged in pairs are known as opposite. Opposite leaves may all face the same way, or each pair may be at right angles to the pair below.

WHERE DID THE FIRST WILD STRAWBERRY GROW?

FACT FILE

Strawberries grow wild or are raised commercially in almost every country. Plant breeders have developed hundreds of varieties of strawberries that are suited for different growing conditions.

Wild strawberries are first recorded in ancient Rome. They have been grown ever since, but the first known hybrid was not developed until the eighteenth century, in France, by crossing varieties from different regions of the Americas.

Strawberries are members of the rose family and are low-growing plants that usually propagate by means of their extensive runners, from which roots extend into the soil. They are not in fact classed as true berries as each of the small yellow 'seeds' on the outside of a strawberry is, in fact, a separate fruit. The 'berries' are pale green when first formed and slowly turn red once they are fully grown.

WHAT IS MADE FROM THE WILLOW TREE?

Willow trees usually live in moist habitats and in floodplains and riverbanks where they grow very rapidly. Their wood is used in many ways, and their leaves supply food for wildlife. Twigs of the common osier are grown for use in basket making, and the light but dent-resistant wood of other willows is used for artificial limbs, wooden shoes and cricket bats.

Willow bark contains the active compound salicin, used in many folk medicines. Aspirin is a derivative of salicylic acid, which was first synthesized from derivatives of willow bark.

FACT FILE

Willow-pattern china originated in Staffordshire, England, c.1780. Thomas Minton, then an apprentice potter, developed and engraved the design, taken from an old Chinese legend.

WHAT IS BARK?

Bark is the outer covering of the stem of woody plants, composed of waterproof cork cells. This protects a layer of food-conducting tissue called the *phloem* or inner bark (also called *bast*). As the woody stem increases in size, the outer bark of dead cork cells gives way – it may split to form grooves, shred, as in the cedar, or peel off, as in the sycamore. A layer of reproductive cells called the cork cambium produces new cork cells to replace or reinforce the old ones. Trees are sometimes damaged by animals that eat the outer bark by cutting through the phloem tubes, this can result in starvation of the roots and, ultimately, the death of the tree. The outer bark of the paper birch was used by Native Americans to make baskets and canoes.

FACT FILE

Bottle corks are made from the thick, spongy bark of the cork oak, which occurs in the Mediterranean region. Oaks produce durable, tough wood and are important lumber trees.

WHAT IS PEAT?

In swamps and marshes, particularly in cold or temperate climates, matter that has fallen from dead plants decays, only very slowly, as there is very little oxygen. Peat is partly decayed plant matter made up of layer upon layer of plants such as reeds, rushes and sedges.

In Ireland, peat is used to generate electricity because other sources such as coal are scarce. Depending on its state of decay and the plants involved, dried peat ranges from a light yellow-brown tangle of plant matter to deep layers of dark brown, compact material that looks like brown coal. Commercially dug peat is removed by machine and used for various purposes – black peat as a fertilizer and light brown peat as bedding for cattle and sheep. Moss peat, which is derived mainly from sphagnum moss is used in agriculture as litter for poultry and horses, as well as a mulch and a soil conditioner. Efforts are being made to find alternatives because of concerns that too much of the peat bogs is being destroyed.

FACT FILE

Peat is the earliest stage of transition from compressed plant growth to the formation of coal. The oldest coal was formed 350 million years ago, and the process still continues in swamps and bogs.

Sphagnum moss

48

WHY DOES A PINE TREE HAVE CONES?

A pine tree has cones in order to reproduce. The pine cone is actually a highly modified branch which takes the place of a flower. Separate male cones and female seed cones are borne on the same tree. Each of the numerous scales of the male cone bears pollen, while each female cone scale bears ovules in which egg cells are produced. In the pine the male cones are small and short-lived and are borne in clusters at the top of the tree. At the time of pollination, enormous numbers of pollen grains are released and dispersed by the wind. Those that land accidentally on female cone scales extend pollen tubes part way into the ovule during one growing season, but usually do not reach the stage of actual fertilization until the next year. The cones that are usually seen are the seed cones, which are normally hard and woody.

FACT FILE

Scots pine trees need to be tough to survive long, cold winters. They have thousands of tiny, needle-like leaves. The needles have a waterproof coating to protect them from the rain and snow.

WHAT ARE STOMATA?

Stomata are tiny holes in leaves, which the plant can open and close. When the stomata are open, they let air in and out, and water out. When the stomata are closed, water cannot escape from the leaves.

Plants absorb water from the soil through their roots. This water moves up the stem to the leaves, where about 90 percent evaporates through the stomata. Large trees lose more than 200 gallons (800 litres) of water from their leaves each day. This loss of water from leaves by evaporation is called transpiration. Other plant processes that involve water include photosynthesis, which uses water to make food, and respiration, in which water is produced. When it is dark, plants shut down for the night by closing stomata.

FACT FILE

Every day, a large tree loses enough water for you to take eight long showers. About 90 per cent of the water absorbed by the roots is lost by the leaves in transpiration.

WHICH IS THE BIGGEST FLOWER OF ALL?

FACT FILE

Green algae are the smallest plants. They form, for example, a greenish film often found on the bark of trees. Millions of cells of algae are needed to cover the tree trunk.

The biggest flower of all is called the *rafflesia*, a parasitic plant that does not photosynthesize. It grows in the rainforests of southeast Asia. The plant actually grows underground and is not visible until a huge bud appears, somewhat like a cabbage. This opens up into a leathery flower which is approximately 3 ft (1 m) across and weighing up to 22 lb (10 kg). The flower is not a pretty sight. It looks and smells just like a huge lump of rotting flesh. It attracts thousands of flies, which pollinate the flower as they walk on it.

HOW DO TREES GROW ?

Tree trunks consist of a number of structures. On the outside is the bark, which is itself divided into two layers, an outer layer called cork and an inner layer known as phloem. The middle of the tree is the wood, or xylem. Between the wood of a tree and the inner bark, there is a thin band of living cells called the cambium, which is where two layers of new cells are formed as wood on the inside and as bark on the outside. In this way, as the tree grows older it increases in diameter.

More living cells grow at the ends of twigs and branches and each year they extend farther, as well as forming leaves and sometimes flowers in the growing season.

When a cross section is cut through a tree alternating bands of light and dark wood are revealed. The lighter bands were formed in the spring and have bigger cells; the dark bands were laid down in the autumn and consist of small, tightly packed cells. Scientists can match tree rings with large databases of similar trees and use these to work out the age of a tree.

FACT FILE

Trees are the largest living organisms on Earth. The biggest tree, the Californian giant redwood, is nearly 300 ft (100 m) high and has a trunk that is 35 ft (11 m) thick. These ancient trees have very few branches and leaves, and are often scarred by forest fires and lightning strikes.

HOW DO LEAVES GROW?

Most green plants, including trees, have to manufacture their food. They do this in their leaves (and in some plants the stems as well) through a process called photosynthesis.

The roots of a plant or tree take water from the soil by capillary action and it eventually reaches the veins of the leaves. Carbon dioxide enters the tree's cells through the stomata in the leaves and when the sun is shining, cells there, called chloroplasts, which contain the green pigment chlorophyll, manufacture sugar, starches and cellulose.

The sugar, starch and cellulose are transported throughout the tree to where they are needed to produce new cells and add sweetness to the fruit.

Oxygen is a by-product of the process and exits the tree through the stomata, together with most of the water that was absorbed by the roots.

FACT FILE

Energy from the Sun evaporates water from the leaf surface, through the stomata. This reduces pressure in the channels carrying water from the roots, so more water is drawn up the stem.

Water evaporates from the leaves' surfaces into the surrounding air

More water is taken up by the roots from the soil

HOW DO FLOWERS DEVELOP THEIR SCENT?

Fragrant flowers contain substances called essential oils in their petals. There are thousands of different types and they are very complex. When these substances are broken down or decomposed, which is a natural process and in the wild is aimed at attracting pollinators, the essential oils become volatile oils, which evaporate, and when this happens we can smell the fragrance the flower gives off. Some plants also have essential oils in other places, for example, citrus fruits contain essential oils in the pith of their fruits and give off strong scents if scratched. Others contain scents in their nuts, bark or roots, such as ginger.

A flower's scent depends on the different chemicals in the volatile oils. Various combinations produce different fragrances.

The Arabians were the first to distil rose petals with water to produce rose water. This was 1,200 years ago, and we still extract perfume from flowers today.

FACT FILE

The hummingbird is the world's smallest bird. It can hover backwards as it feeds on flower nectar.

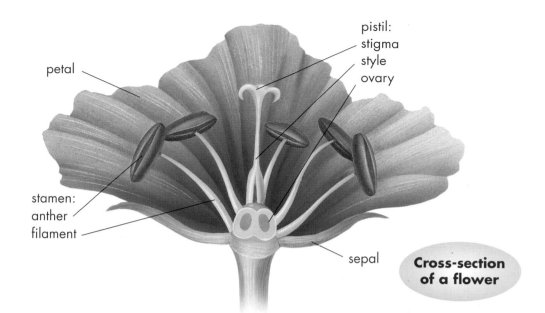

petal

pistil:
stigma
style
ovary

stamen:
anther
filament

sepal

Cross-section of a flower

WHAT HAPPENS IN FLOWERS?

Flowers come in many different shapes and sizes, but most contain the same four main parts, although these may not look the same in different flowers. In a 'normal' flower the sepals make up a green outer cup, and within the sepals are the petals, which are often coloured. In the middle of the flower are one or more pistils, which form the female part of the flower. The bottom of this area is enlarged to form the ovary, which contains little round ovules, which will later form into seeds if they are fertilized by the contents of a pollen grain from another flower. Pollen is produced by the stamens, the male organs of the flower and to fuse with an egg cell a grain must land on the stigma and develop into a tube to reach the ovules at the bottom of the pistil. Pollen can be carried by wind or by insects feeding on nectar and moving from plant to plant.

FACT FILE

Pollen is the plant's equivalent of an animal's sperm. It carries the male reproductive genes. Pollen grains have a pattern, allowing the plant to be identified.

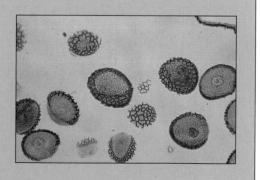

WHY DO PINE TREES STAY GREEN ALL YEAR?

In most trees, leaves give off enormous amounts of water. In fact, in some, more than 90 per cent of the water absorbed by the roots and transported to the leaves is lost through evaporation. For most broad-leaved trees, such as oak, chestnuts, ash and maples this would be impossible to sustain in winter when the ground is frozen and they would die through lack of water. So these deciduous trees drop their leaves in autumn to protect themselves. Certain trees, however, like pines and firs have developed another strategy to avoid drying out. Their leaves are needlelike and covered in a waxy layer that prevents evaporation. They do not need to drop their leaves in autumn because their water requirements are low. When individual leaves do fall, new ones replace them and the branches never look bare.

Corsican Pine

Norway Spruce

FACT FILE

Fertilizers are used to make crops grow larger and faster. Crops are also regularly sprayed with pesticides and herbicides. There are fears that the chemicals could cause health problems.

WHAT ARE PERENNIAL PLANTS?

Daffodil

Perennial plants survive from one year to the next. They usually grow quite slowly, and can afford to build up their strength before they need to produce seeds. The parts of perennial plants that are above the ground are generally killed by frost in the autumn, but the roots and/or underground parts live through the winter. Growth is renewed and the cycle begins anew in the spring.

Perennial plants that grow in arid or desert conditions commonly survive dry times by becoming physiologically inactive. In some cases they remain alive but are dehydrated until water becomes available, at which time they rapidly absorb moisture through above-ground parts, swelling and resuming physiological activity. Some plants can absorb dew, which for many is the main water source. Mosses and lichens adopt this strategy, as do some flowering plants, which are sometimes called resurrection plants.

FACT FILE

As well as looking very like small bees, the flowers of bee orchids actually produce a female bee 'smell'. They are therefore highly attractive to male bees.

WHAT IS POISON IVY?

Poison ivy is a harmful vine or shrub, which is a member of the cashew family. It is widespread in southern Canada and parts of the United States. The plant's tissues contain a poisonous oil, which is similar to carbolic acid and highly irritating to the skin. Although poison ivy usually grows as a vine, climbing up trees or wandering across the soil, it will form a shrubby habit if there is no support available.

In early spring, the leaves are red, and by late spring, they change to shiny green. Then, in autumn they turn back to red or orange. Each leaf is composed of three leaflets with notched edges. Later in the season, clusters of whitish, waxy drupes that resemble berries form. These are just as poisonous as the leaves.

FACT FILE

Ground ivy is a member of the mint family and is not closely related to true ivies or poison ivy. It has a trailing habit and sends creeping stems across the ground, and forms mats of leaves where it takes hold.

Earth & Space

HOW CAN A DAY BE DEFINED? 60
WHAT IS A HEMISPHERE? 61

HOW DEEP IS THE PACIFIC OCEAN? 62
WHAT CAUSES TIDES? 63

WHAT ARE OCEAN TRENCHES? 64
WHAT ARE CURRENTS? 65

HOW DID THE CONTINENTS USE TO LOOK? 66
WHAT IS PLATE TECTONICS? 67

WHAT SHAPE IS THE SEA-FLOOR? 68
WHAT ARE CONTINENTAL SHELVES? 69

WHY DOES LAND EROSION OCCUR? 70
WHAT ERODES THE DESERTS? 71

WHY DO GLACIERS FORM? 72
WHAT IS AN ICE SHEET? 73

WHAT SHAPES A RIVER? 74
WHAT SHAPES THE COASTS? 75

WHAT IS CLIMATE? 76
WHAT IS A SAVANNA? 77

WHAT IS THE WATER CYCLE? 78
WHY DOES FLOODING OCCUR? 79

WHAT IS ACID RAIN? 80
WHY DOES DEFORESTATION OCCUR? 81

HOW BIG ARE ASTEROIDS? 82
HOW ARE METEORITES FORMED? 83

HOW MUCH DOES THE ATMOSPHERE WEIGH? 84
HOW OLD IS THE EARTH? 85

HOW ARE STARS FORMED? 86
HOW FAR AWAY ARE THE STARS? 87

HOW FAST DOES THE EARTH MOVE? 88

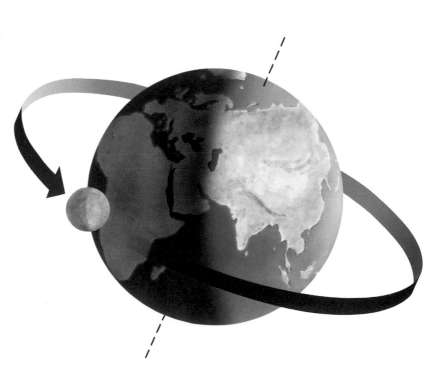

HOW CAN A DAY BE DEFINED?

For early people, the only changes that were truly regular, were the motions of objects in the sky. The most obvious of these changes was the alternate daylight and darkness, caused by the rising and setting of the Sun. Each of these cycles of the Sun came to be called a day. Another regular change in the sky was the change in the visible shape of the Moon. Each cycle of the Moon's changing shape takes about 29½ days, or a month. The cycle of the seasons gave people an even longer unit of time.

There is no regular change in the sky that lasts seven days, to represent the week. The seven-day week came from the Jewish custom of observing a Sabbath (day of rest) every seventh day. The division of a day into 24 hours, an hour into 60 minutes, and a minute into 60 seconds probably came from the ancient Babylonians.

FACT FILE

Some clock faces are divided into 24 hours. On such a clock, 9 a.m. would be shown as 0900 and 4 p.m. would be 1600. This system avoids confusion between the morning and evening hours.

21 JUNE — North Pole: 24 hours daylight

13.5 hours daylight

SUN'S RAYS

12 hours daylight

10.5 hours daylight

South Pole: 24 hours darkness

WHAT IS A HEMISPHERE?

FACT FILE

The equator is an imaginary line drawn around the outside of the Earth. It divides the Earth into two halves, called hemispheres. It was invented by mapmakers because it makes a convenient point from which to measure distances north and south.

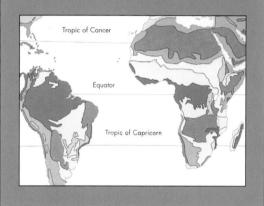

Tropic of Cancer

Equator

Tropic of Capricorn

A hemisphere is the name given to any half of any globe, including the Earth. It is derived from the Greek for half a sphere.

For convenience, geographers divide the Earth into hemispheres with the equator as a boundary. Everything north of the equator is in the Northern Hemisphere, while everything to south lies in the Southern Hemisphere. The equator lies at an equal distance from the geographic north and south poles.

Because land is not distributed evenly across the surface of the Earth, the globe may also be divided into land and water hemispheres, the former centred near London and the latter near New Zealand.

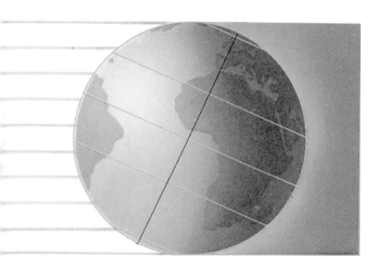

HOW DEEP IS THE PACIFIC OCEAN?

The Pacific Ocean, the largest and deepest of the world's four oceans, covers more than a third of the Earth's surface and contains more than half of its free water. The floor of the Pacific Ocean, which has an average depth of around 14,000 feet (4,300 m), is largely a deep-sea plain. The name Pacific, which means peaceful, was given to it by the Portuguese navigator Ferdinand Magellan in 1520. The Pacific is the oldest of the existing ocean basins, its oldest rocks having been dated at 200 million years.

The Pacific Ocean is bounded on the east by the North and South American continents; on the north by the Bering Strait; on the west by Asia, the Malay Archipelago, and Australia; and on the south by Antarctica.

360 million sq km of Earth's surface is covered by water

FACT FILE

The Pacific Ocean contains more than 30,000 islands; their total land area, however, amounts to only one-quarter of one percent of the ocean's surface area.

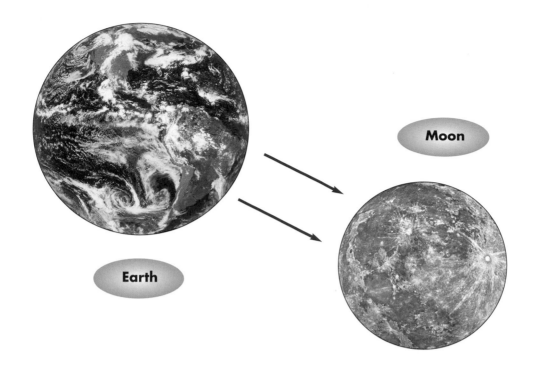

Moon

Earth

WHAT CAUSES TIDES?

The daily rise and fall of the ocean's tides occur because of the pull of gravity of the Moon. As the Earth spins round, the water in the oceans is 'pulled' towards the Moon slightly, making a bulge. There is a corresponding bulge on the other side of the Earth. Wherever the bulges are positioned it is high tide. In between, the water is shallower and so it is low tide. High tides occur every 25 hours, because at the same time that the Earth is spinning on its axis, the Moon is travelling around the Earth once every 27½ days. This means that high tides are about one hour later every day.

FACT FILE

Spring tides are tides with unusually high ranges which occur twice each month when the Sun, Earth, and Moon are in line. They can be especially high in the spring and autumn.

WHAT ARE OCEAN TRENCHES?

FACT FILE

For centuries, most people assumed that the cold, black depths of the ocean supported little or no life. Scientists have since discovered a great variety of living things in the deep sea.

Trenches are the deepest parts of the ocean. Many trenches occur in the Pacific Ocean, especially in its western portion. Most trenches are long, narrow, and deep, 2 to 2.5 miles (3 to 4 km) below the surrounding sea floor. The greatest depth anywhere in the ocean is found in the Mariana Trench southeast of Japan. It plunges more than 6.8 miles (11 km) below sea level. Frequent earthquakes and volcanic eruptions occur along the trenches because they are where oceanic crust is being forced underneath continental crust.

Deep-sea fish are very different from those found in shallow waters

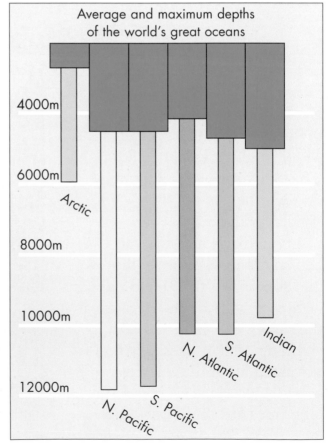

Average and maximum depths of the world's great oceans

Arctic
N. Pacific
S. Pacific
N. Atlantic
S. Atlantic
Indian

WHAT ARE CURRENTS?

The oceans are moved by the wind on their surface and from the movement inside the ocean. Ocean currents can move a large amount of heat around the Earth and can control the climate. The way the water circulates depends on the spinning of the Earth. The water in the Northern Hemisphere spins clockwise and the water in the Southern Hemisphere spins anti-clockwise. The ocean currents are different in summer and winter. The wind direction can change which ocean current will be influencing the weather in a country. A cold ocean current can make the weather cold, while a warm ocean current can make the weather warm.

FACT FILE

A whirlpool is a mass of water which spins around and around rapidly and with great force. It may occur when opposing currents meet, or it may be caused by the action of the wind.

Ocean currents

Summer in Northern Hemisphere

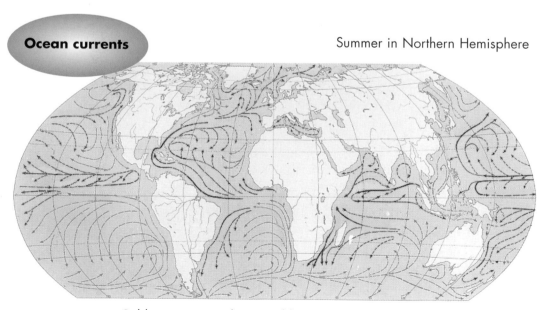

Cold currents are shown in blue, warm currents in red

200 million years ago

135 million years ago

Present day

150 million years' time

HOW DID THE CONTINENTS USED TO LOOK?

When the Earth formed, the lighter elements floated to the surface where they cooled to form a crust. Although the first rocks were formed over 3,500 years ago they have not stayed the same. They have been changed from forces on the inside and the outside of the Earth. The coastlines on each side of the Atlantic appear to have a jigsaw fit. It is thought that all the land masses were once joined together, forming a super continent called Pangaea. This split up to form the continents we know today.

FACT FILE

Movement of the land is still taking place as India and Asia are colliding, forming the Himalayas. This is called continental drift.

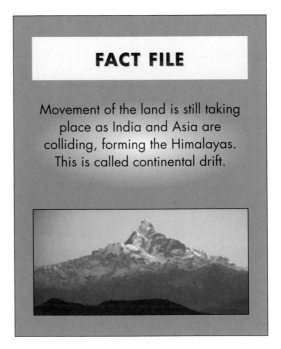

WHAT IS PLATE TECTONICS?

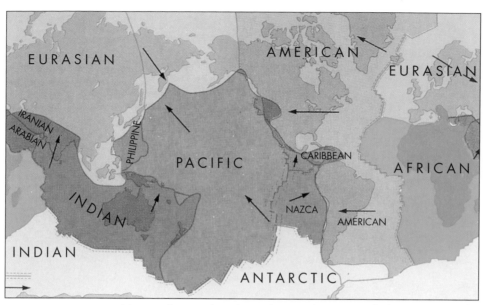

EURASIAN

AMERICAN

EURASIAN

IRANIAN

ARABIAN

PHILIPPINE

PACIFIC

CARIBBEAN

AFRICAN

INDIAN

NAZCA

AMERICAN

INDIAN

ANTARCTIC

Major plates, plate boundaries, direction of plate movements

Plate tectonics theory explains the major features of the Earth's surface, both on land and under the oceans – how mountains are formed, what is happening in deep-sea trenches and why earthquakes and volcanoes occur where they do. The Earth's crust is broken into fragments, called plates, of varying sizes and these are moving in response to currents in the slowly flowing, but solid, mantle rock beneath. The plates move at different speeds, ranging from ½ to 4 inches (1 to 10 cm) a year. Scientists make these measurements by bouncing lasers from various points on the Earth from reflectors left on the Moon by Apollo astronauts and work out the relative difference and direction of motion.

FACT FILE

The plates have been moving about slowly on the Earth's surface for hundreds of millions of years and will continue to do so, building mountain chains and creating new oceans, both forming and destroying land as they go.

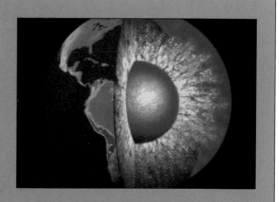

WHAT SHAPES THE SEA-FLOOR?

The bottom of the ocean has features as varied as those on land. Huge plains spread out across the ocean floor, and long mountain chains rise toward the surface. Volcanoes erupt from the ocean bottom, and deep valleys cut through the floor. In the early 1960s, a theory called sea-floor spreading provided an explanation. According to the theory, the circulating currents deep within the mantle pull the the sea-floor apart, carrying the continents with it. Molten magma is forced by pressure up into central valleys of the mid-ocean ridges. The magma cools and hardens to form new sea-floor and pushes older floor away. At the edges of the plate, some of the old oceanic crust dives under the continents.

FACT FILE

A hot vent is a chimney-like structure on the ocean floor that discharges hot, mineral-rich water. Scientists first observed hot vents in 1977, in the Galapagos Rift, a region on the floor of the Pacific Ocean.

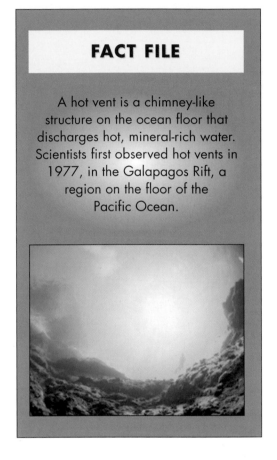

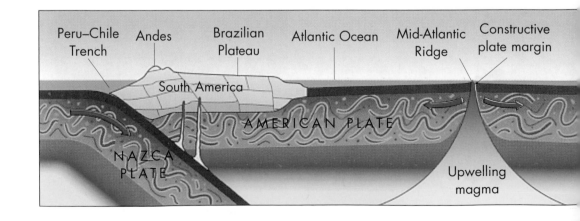

Peru–Chile Trench · Andes · Brazilian Plateau · Atlantic Ocean · Mid-Atlantic Ridge · Constructive plate margin · South America · AMERICAN PLATE · NAZCA PLATE · Upwelling magma

WHAT ARE CONTINENTAL SHELVES?

The continental margin is the area that separates the part of a continent above sea level from the deep sea floor. It consists of three parts, the continental shelf, the continental slope, and the continental rise.

The continental shelf begins at the shoreline and gently slopes underwater to an average depth of about 440 ft (135 m). The width of the continental shelf averages 47 miles (75 km), although in some places it is thousands of miles across and in others only a few feet. Valleys of varying depths cut through the shelf. At the edge of the continental shelf, there is an abrupt change in steepness, and the continental slope plunges down to the continental rise or, in some cases, to ocean trenches.

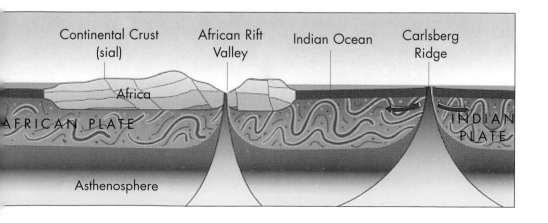

Continental Crust (sial)

African Rift Valley

Indian Ocean

Carlsberg Ridge

Africa

AFRICAN PLATE

INDIAN PLATE

Asthenosphere

WHY DOES LAND EROSION OCCUR?

Erosion is a process through which rock and soil are broken loose from the Earth's surface in one place and moved elsewhere. Natural erosion alters the shape of the land by wearing down mountains, filling in valleys and rivers with sediment. It is usually a slow process that makes little difference in thousands of years. Erosion begins with weathering, through the action of rain and snow, rivers, wind and ice, including glaciers. Sediments are eventually carried down from the mountains to the plains below, creating fertile land. If soil is left bare, rain and wind will wash it into streams and rivers and it will eventually be washed out to sea and end up on the ocean floor.

FACT FILE

Erosion can be speeded up by such human activities as farming and forestry. Landslides are one catastrophic result of too much supporting vegetation being lost.

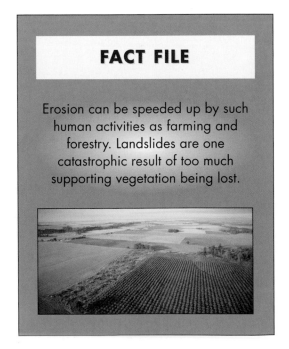

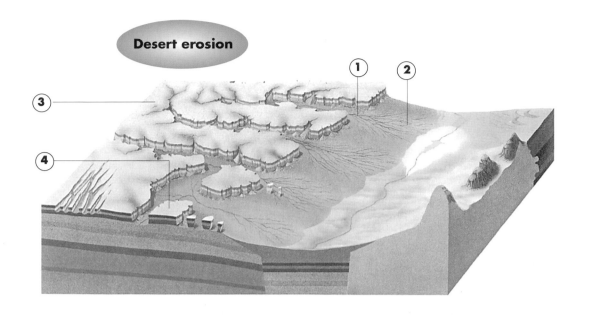

Desert erosion

③

④

① ②

WHAT ERODES THE DESERTS?

A dry desert landscape includes surface features that have been created over thousands of years through erosion by wind and the ensuing deposit of silt and sand. After rain, water fills usually dry stream channels called wadis ①. The rapidly flowing water cuts into the soft rocks of desert mountains and carries sediments down through canyons and deposits sediments in fan-shaped forms known as alluvial fans ②.

Sometimes, the streams carry large amounts of water out into low areas in the desert plains that form temporary lakes. The water that collects in these lakes either evaporates or seeps into the ground. Water erosion in deserts also creates big flat-topped hills known as mesas ③ and smaller flat-topped hills called buttes ④.

Sand dunes are not fixed features but move with the prevailing wind.

FACT FILE

Vast regions covered by sand and dunes are called sand seas. Sand seas cover large areas in desert regions of Africa, Asia, and Australia.

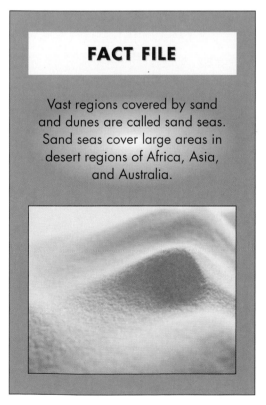

WHY DO GLACIERS FORM?

glacier

debris carried
by glacier

deposited debris

Glaciers begin to form on mountains when the winter snow fall outweighs the summer snowmelt and evaporation. The excess snow builds up in layers over years. The increasing weight of successive layers of snow compresses the crystals below the surface, eventually turning them into dense, blue glacial ice. The glacier becomes so massive that it moves down the mountain slope under the influence of gravity, gouging out rock from the sides and floor of the valley. The top of the glacier continues to be fed with fresh snow.

FACT FILE

Glaciers have shaped most of the world's highest mountains, carving out huge valleys. Lakes in mountain regions are formed from flooded glacial valleys that become dammed by debris as the glacier melts.

WHAT IS AN ICE SHEET?

Over 10,000 years ago about a third of the land surface was covered by ice. Today a tenth is still covered in ice. Ice sheets can cover very large areas and can be very thick. The world's largest ice sheet covers most of Antarctica and is very slow moving.

Antarctica covers about 5,400,000 square miles (14,000,000 square km). It is larger in area than either Europe or Australia. However, Antarctica would be the smallest continent if it did not have its ice cap. This icy layer, which averages approximately 7,100 feet (2,200 m) thick, increases Antarctica's surface area and also makes Antarctica the highest continent in terms of average elevation.

FACT FILE

Glaciers and ice sheets sometimes give up their secrets centuries later. Thawing ice has revealed the bodies of people who fell into crevasses hundreds of years ago. The ice preserved their clothes and their internal organs.

WHAT SHAPES A RIVER?

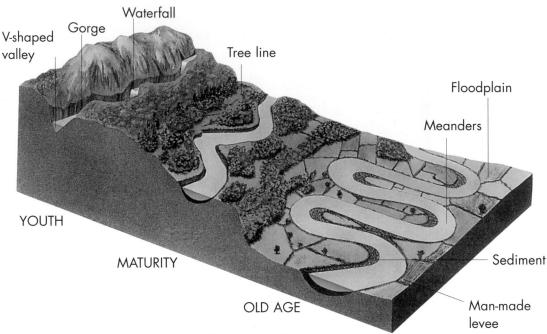

V-shaped valley

Gorge

Waterfall

Tree line

Floodplain

Meanders

YOUTH

MATURITY

OLD AGE

Sediment

Man-made levee

Rivers start on the top of hills as small streams channelling the rainfall or as a spring releasing ground water. They begin to cut at and change the landscape on the way to the sea. In the highlands the water can move very quickly and has a lot of power. The river can cut deep gorges and V-shaped valleys in the softer rocks. In the harder rocks they can form waterfalls. The river moves rocks and pebbles along its bed by bouncing and rolling. The lighter sediments are carried or dissolved in the water. When they reach the more gentle slopes the river becomes wider and moves slower. Mud and sand is dropped when the river floods and forms ridges along the river bank. When the river reaches the low plains it begins to meander.

FACT FILE

The farther a river is from its source on a mountainside, the slower the water travels. This is because the river eventually reaches flatter ground and widens before it reaches the sea.

WHAT SHAPES THE COASTS?

FACT FILE

Many cliffs on the coast are made up of chalk. Chalk is formed from the skeletons of millions and millions of tiny animals called foraminifera. It is a sedimentary rock that formed millions of years ago beneath shallow seas.

Coastlines are constantly changing: they are either being eroded or built up. The waves are very powerful and can remove a large amount of material from a coastline, especially during a storm. The sand and pebbles removed from the coastline are carried by the sea and can be dropped farther along a coast or out at sea.

Many coastal features can be made by the steady erosion of the cliffs and headlands such as sand dunes, spits and salt marshes. A beach can make the waves less powerful and reduce the amount of erosion of the coast. Steep cliffs and wave-cut platforms can be formed in areas of hard rock. A bay can be carved out in an area where hard rock has soft rock between it.

SOFT ROCK

Cliff

HARD ROCK

Wave-cut platform

Wave-built terrace

HARD AND SOFT ROCK

Cove

Headland

Arch

Stack

WHAT IS CLIMATE?

FACT FILE

Mountains, such as the Rockies in North America, have a typical alpine climate because of their height.

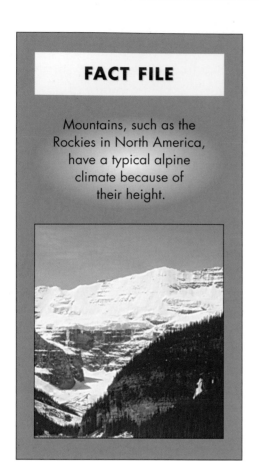

Climatic zones

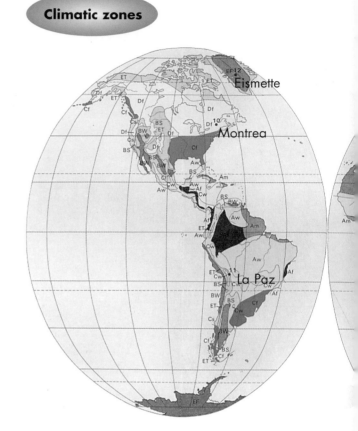

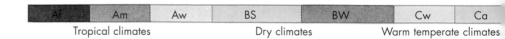

Af	Am	Aw	BS	BW	Cw	Ca
Tropical climates			Dry climates		Warm temperate climates	

Climate is what the weather pattern is like over a long time. The seasonal pattern of hot and cold, wet or dry, is averaged over 30 years. The climate is different around the world as it is not heated evenly by the Sun. The equator gets most of the heat. Winds and ocean currents transport the heat around the Earth.

There are four types of climate: these are tropical, desert (dry), temperate, and polar.

Different areas of the world have different weather patterns. Some areas have a high level of rainfall while others remain dry. Throughout a year the weather in a country may change with the seasons.

WHAT IS A SAVANNA?

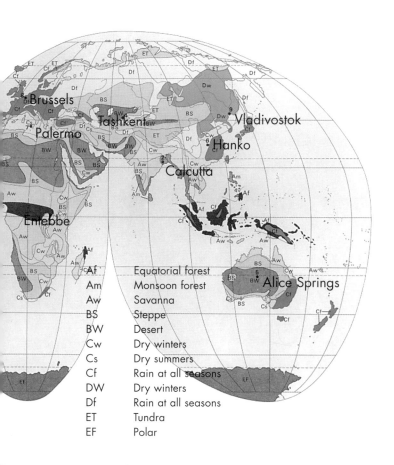

Af	Equatorial forest
Am	Monsoon forest
Aw	Savanna
BS	Steppe
BW	Desert
Cw	Dry winters
Cs	Dry summers
Cf	Rain at all seasons
DW	Dry winters
Df	Rain at all seasons
ET	Tundra
EF	Polar

Cf	Dw	Df	ET	EF
Cool temperate climates			Cold climates	

FACT FILE

As well as grazing animals, the African savanna is home to animals that prey on them, such as lions and cheetahs, as well as birds, insects and reptiles.

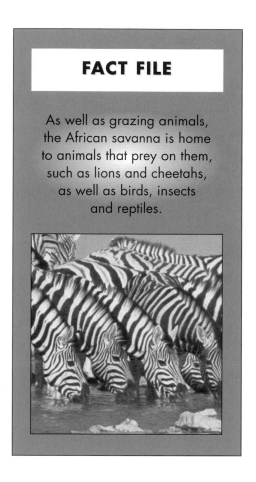

Savannas are grasslands in areas that have both dry and rainy seasons, and tend to lie between rain forests and deserts, with widely scattered trees and shrubs. Most savannas are in the tropics and they cover more than 40 per cent of Africa as well as large areas of India, central South America and northern Australia. Trees and shrubs are widely scattered on savannas and their growth is limited by the dry season, during which no rain may fall for nearly half a year. When the dry season begins, most trees drop their leaves to conserve water and the clumpy grasses die back. Grazing animals, such as zebras and wildebeest migrate across the savanna to follow the available water.

WHAT IS THE WATER CYCLE?

In nature, all the world's water circulates from the oceans to the sky, onto the land and then back to the oceans in what is called the water cycle or hydrological cycle. Heat from the sun evaporates water from the oceans, which gradually rises as vapour in the atmosphere. The vaporized water gradually cools and condenses to form clouds, which will deposit water back in the oceans or on the land as rain or snow. The majority falls directly back onto the oceans or seas, but some falls on the land and flows back to the seas, completing the cycle, sometimes after periods of thousands of years.

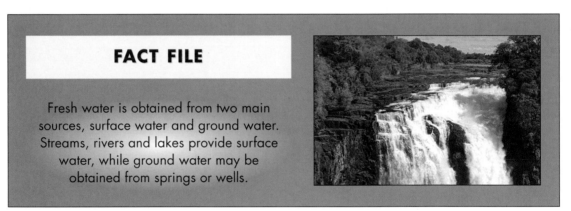

FACT FILE

Fresh water is obtained from two main sources, surface water and ground water. Streams, rivers and lakes provide surface water, while ground water may be obtained from springs or wells.

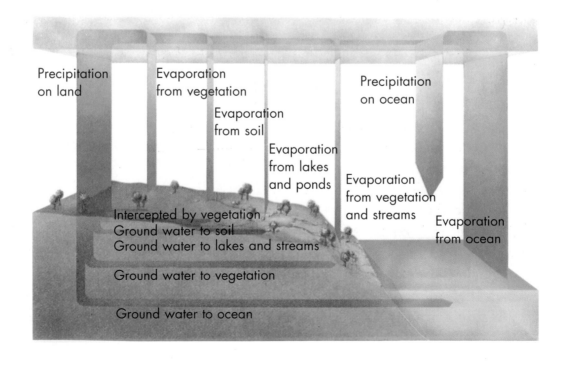

Precipitation on land

Evaporation from vegetation

Evaporation from soil

Precipitation on ocean

Evaporation from lakes and ponds

Evaporation from vegetation and streams

Intercepted by vegetation
Ground water to soil
Ground water to lakes and streams

Evaporation from ocean

Ground water to vegetation

Ground water to ocean

WHY DOES FLOODING OCCUR?

Flooding occurs when water cannot drain away fast enough in the rivers. In areas of non-porous rocks, water runs off the land very quickly and streams and rivers soon overflow. Flooding also happens when winter snows thaw in spring. Huge floods cover parts of Siberia every spring, when snow melts while the rivers are still iced up. Low-lying coastal lands are vulnerable to flooding, especially when gales and high tides cause water to flow inland. Low-lying Bangladesh is particularly liable to this kind of flooding. In addition, melting snow in the Himalayan mountains adds huge amounts of water to Bangladesh's rivers, increasing the flood risk.

FACT FILE

Many of the world's cities are low lying and threatened by flooding. Bangkok, in Thailand, and Venice, in Italy, are typical old cities built near water because they relied on shipping.

WHAT IS ACID RAIN?

FACT FILE

Attempts have been made to neutralize the acidity of some lakes by adding lime, but it is not known whether this may have harmful side effects.

Acid rain is rain, snow or sleet that has been polluted by acids. Increased acidity upsets the delicate pH balance of fresh water and kills insects, fish and other wildlife that depend on lakes, rivers and streams. High concentrations of acid rain can harm forests, burning the trees leaves and changing the acidity of soil, making it difficult for plants to thrive. They become less resistant to disease and many die.

Acid rain is a problem of the industrial age, resulting mainly from the burning of fossil fuels in power stations and factories as well as cars and other vehicles. The resulting compounds, for example sulphur dioxide and nitrogen oxides, react with vapour in the atmosphere to create such compounds as sulphuric and nitric acid.

Large parts of eastern North America, central Europe, Scandinavia and parts of Asia are badly affected by the effects of acid rain. Acts forcing companies to reduce their emissions of such compounds have been in force in many western countries for some years now and the levels of acidity are beginning to drop. However, this improvement is not yet happening worldwide.

WHY DOES DEFORESTATION OCCUR?

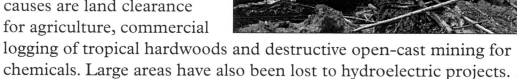

The world's rainforests are disappearing rapidly. More than half of their area has been irretrievably destroyed by humans. The primary causes are land clearance for agriculture, commercial logging of tropical hardwoods and destructive open-cast mining for chemicals. Large areas have also been lost to hydroelectric projects.

In the last few years of the twentieth century, forest clearance in Indonesia caused extensive forest fires; the smoke blanketed much of Southeast Asia for some months.

Worryingly, rainforest species such as the orang-utan are in danger of extinction because of the destruction of their habitat. Most animals die when people clear large areas of forest, leaving only isolated patches that are not large enough for them to live in. More than 7,000 species, including insects, reptiles and mammals are thought to become extinct each year.

FACT FILE

Rain forests benefit people in four major ways. They provide (1) economic, (2) scientific, (3) environmental, and (4) recreational value.

HOW BIG ARE ASTEROIDS?

Asteroids are small rocky or icy bodies that orbit the Sun. There are over 100,000 in orbit and some measure less than ½ a mile (1 km) across, while the largest known is 630 miles (1,000 km) in size and only a few of them have a diameter of more than 19 miles (30 km). They are sometimes called minor planets. Most asteroids are found in an orbit between Mars and Jupiter, called the asteroid belt, and more than 7,000 of these have been identified. The asteroid belt may be the shattered remains of a planet destroyed by Jupiter's enormous gravity, or perhaps one that was prevented from forming. There are also asteroids in orbits near the Earth, as well as in the same orbit as Jupiter.

One asteroid, called Ida, has a tiny moon of its own, Dactyl, and is the smallest known body in the solar system to have a satellite. Astronomers believe that the asteroids were probably formed, at the same time as the planets, from the dust cloud that surrounded the Sun when it was young.

The Asteroid Belt

FACT FILE

Many asteroids have struck the Earth already, although the resulting craters have been covered by geological activity. Many scientists believe that such an impact off Mexico 65 million years ago caused the extinction of the dinosaurs.

HOW ARE METEORITES FORMED?

Meteorites are made of rock or metal. They may have been formed at the same time as the solar system, or may be debris from impacts between other small bodies and planets such as Mars. They enter the Earth's atmosphere at speeds of at least 6.9 mps (11 kms), which makes them glow as they vaporize. Several thousand meteoroids enter the Earth's atmosphere every year, but very few reach the ground. Technically, meteoroids are only called meteorites if they actually hit the planet. The largest known meteorite is made of iron and weighs 65 tons (66 tonnes). It probably fell to the Earth in prehistoric times in Namibia, southwest Africa.

It is very hard to find meteorites. Recently, researchers have been finding them on the ice sheets in the Arctic and the Antarctic, where they are easier to locate.

On planets and moons with no atmosphere, huge numbers of meteorites strike with enormous power. Our own Moon is estimated to have 3,000,000 meteorite craters measuring 1 mile (2 km) or more in diameter. However, meteorite craters are rare on Earth because the atmosphere slows the meteoroid and usually burns it up.

FACT FILE

An enormous meteorite caused this huge impact crater at Wolf Creek in Australia. The amount of energy the impact released would have been equivalent to hundreds of nuclear weapons.

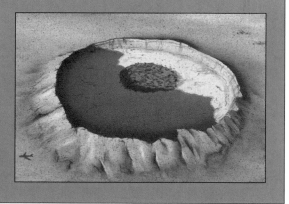

HOW MUCH DOES THE ATMOSPHERE WEIGH?

The Earth is surrounded by a thick blanket of about 20 gases, mainly nitrogen and oxygen, called the atmosphere. It also contains water vapour and dust particles. It is densest closest to the ground and thins progressively with increasing height.

Air, like all matter, has weight. Scientists have calculated that our atmosphere weighs 5,100,000,000,000,000 tons (5,170,000,000,000,000 tonnes)!

So why don't we feel the weight of all this air pressing down on us and against us? Something like a ton of air is pressing against you at this very moment, and yet you are not aware of this because your body is made to live with this pressure. Higher up in the atmosphere, pressure is less, which is why aircraft cabins have to be pressurized. Similarly, pressure increases rapidly with depth in the oceans, and divers can reach only the very top levels of the water without the protection of submarines.

The Earth's atmosphere is one of the most important things that allows it to support life. Chemicals in it protect us from the Sun's rays, it prevents all but the biggest meteorites hitting the surface, without it the oceans would evaporate and, of course, it provides oxygen for us to breathe.

FACT FILE

Beneath the land and water that cover the Earth's surface lie layers of rock and metal at very high temperatures. The deepest mines ever dug have not reached the bottom of the outer layer, called the crust. Under the crust is a layer of partly solid and partly molten rock.

HOW OLD IS THE EARTH?

The Earth began to form over 4.5 billion years ago, but for millions of years nothing could live here. About 3.6 billion years ago, scientists think that a body the size of Mars crashed into the young Earth, resulting in the formation of the Moon. Gradually, the Earth's crust and the oceans and atmosphere formed. But how do we know this? The Earth's geological record does not go back that far, so the answer is based on theory.

To find the age of the Earth it was necessary to find out how the Sun and all the planets came into being.

The first theory is the 'nebular hypothesis', which dates to the eighteenth century. In this theory a mass of white-hot gas whirled about in space getting smaller and hotter all the time, throwing off rings of gas, which condensed to form a planet. The second theory, the 'planetismal hypothesis' dates to the 1920s. In this, the gravitation of a large star pulled on the Sun and caused it to eject filaments of plasma that condensed into tiny bodies, which eventually accreted into planets. The current theory is that as the Sun formed, a broad disk of dust and gas condensed around it. Material within this disk began to clump together and eventually accreted into the nine planets. One way of estimating the Earth's age involves calculating how long it would take for the Moon to acquire the number of craters it has.

FACT FILE

No one has ever proved that life exists on other planets. However, as there are billions of stars, some with planets, it seems unlikely that Earth is the only place with the right conditions for life. Astronomers use radio telescopes to search for messages from other civilizations.

HOW ARE STARS FORMED?

A star is a huge ball of bright, hot ionized gas called plasma. The main source of fuel for most of a star's life is hydrogen, which they convert into helium. They also contain other chemical elements such as nitrogen, oxygen, iron, nickel and zinc.

Stars come into existence in the vast, cold clouds of dust and gas that astronomers refer to as stellar nurseries. They are not particularly dense, but are a lot denser than the vacuum of space. If there is a disturbance in a bit of the cloud, perhaps as the result of a nearby star exploding, some of the particles might clump together. As they do, they will spin together and slowly attract more particles. As the group gradually gets larger and larger, its spins faster and its gravitational attraction becomes greater.

Pressure also builds up within the ball, which increases its heat. Eventually, when the pressure and temperature inside the ball become very high, about 15 million°C, nuclear reactions take place in the core and the gas ball becomes a star. The larger a star, the faster it will use up its hydrogen and some massive stars last only tens of thousands of years before exploding. Small stars like our Sun, last for tens of millions of years.

FACT FILE

A nebula is an enormous mass of gas and material that appears to be solid. However, it is mostly composed of dust and gas, which slowly condenses into stars.

How far away are the stars?

The Sun is about 93,000,000 miles from Earth and as light travels at the rate of 186,000 mps (299,792,458 kms) it takes eight minutes for the light to reach us. The next closest stars to Earth are Proxima Centauri and Alpha Centauri. They are 270,000 times farther away from the Earth than the Sun, so this means that it would take their light 4½ years to reach the Earth. Others are unimaginably far away: Betelgeuse, the red star in Orion's shoulder is approximately 427 light-years away.

To measure the distance of very nearby stars, astronomers use a form of geometry. Close stars appear to move very slightly against the background stars over the Earth's annual orbit, and if measurements are taken at each extreme, perhaps in December and June, the angle between the two points can be used to calculate its distance.

Other techniques are used for measuring the distances to more remote stars and galaxies, involving the use of spectroscopy, the analysis of the chemistry of stars through their light.

FACT FILE

The Milky Way is a huge mass of gas and stars that can be clearly seen as a band of light across the night sky. The Earth, and everything else in the solar system, is part of the Milky Way.

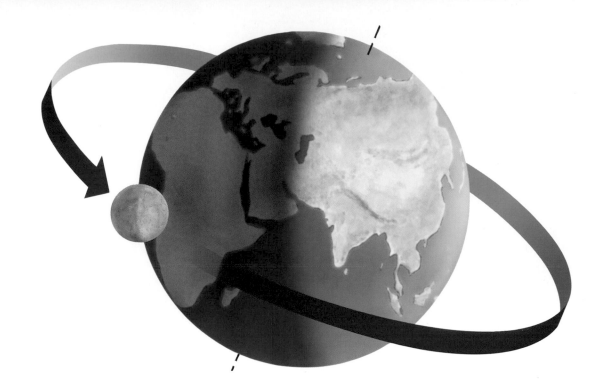

HOW FAST DOES THE EARTH MOVE?

The Earth has two main motions – it spins on its axis once every 23 hours, 56 minutes and 4.091 seconds and it moves in an orbit around the Sun once every 365¼ days.

It was believed that the speed of the rotation never changed, but there are tiny variations and our day is getting longer by about one-thousandth of a second per century.

Like all of the planets, the Earth moves faster when it is closer to the Sun (perihelion) than it does when farther out (aphelion). At aphelion the Earth orbits the Sun at 18.2 mps (29.12 kms) and at perihelion it is travelling at a speed of 18.8 mps (30.8 kms).

FACT FILE

Humans have a built-in body clock and normally have a good idea of the time even without the use of clocks, because our body is aware of the amount of time that has passed since daybreak.

Prehistory

HOW ARE PREHISTORIC TIMES CATEGORIZED? 90
WHAT HAVE WE LEARNT FROM PREHISTORY? 91

HOW ARE FOSSILS FORMED? 92
HOW ARE FOSSILS FOUND? 93

HOW DID LIFE BEGIN ON LAND? 94
WHY DID SOME FISH BECOME LAND-DWELLERS? 95

HOW DO WE KNOW WHAT DINOSAURS WERE LIKE? 96
HOW DID DINOSAURS EVOLVE? 97

HOW MANY DIFFERENT TYPES OF DINOSAUR WERE THERE? 98
HOW BIG WERE DINOSAURS? 99

HOW DID CARNIVOROUS DINOSAURS CATCH THEIR PREY? 100
HOW DID PLANT-EATING DINOSAURS FIND FOOD? 101

DID DINOSAURS LOOK AFTER THEIR YOUNG? 102
HOW BIG WERE DINOSAUR EGGS? 103

HOW DID DINOSAURS PROTECT THEMSELVES? 104
HOW DID DINOSAURS USE THEIR ARMOUR? 105

HOW DID FISH EVOLVE? 106
WHAT DID MARINE REPTILES LOOK LIKE? 107

WHAT SIZE WERE PTEROSAURS? 108
HOW DID PTEROSAURS FLY? 109

WHY DID THE DINOSAURS DIE OUT? 110
DID CLIMATE AFFECT THE DINOSAURS' SURVIVAL? 111

HOW DID MAMMALS EVOLVE? 112
 ARE MARSUPIALS SIMILAR TO THE FIRST MAMMALS? 113

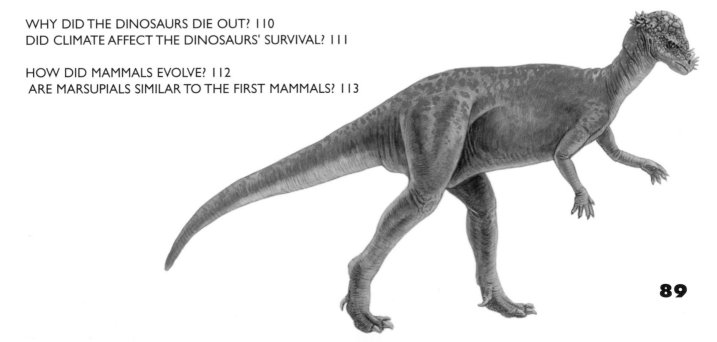

HOW ARE PREHISTORIC TIMES CATEGORIZED?

Geological time covers many millions of years and it has been divided up into eras, which are periods of time identified by the fossilized forms of life from that period. The oldest era, called the Palaeozoic, contains fossils ranging from many primitive life forms up to some of the earliest land-dwelling animals. During this era fishes, amphibians and early reptiles appeared.

The Mesozoic era was the age of giant reptiles, when dinosaurs stalked the world. The Cenozoic era in which we still live is the age of mammals and birds. All fossils can be placed in these eras, which are subdivided further into smaller periods as shown on the chart here.

FACT FILE

Now the habits of dinosaurs are becoming better understood, museums are able to mount their fossilized remains in realistic poses that show people how they lived.

Era	Period	Million years
Cenozoic	Quaternary	1.64
Cenozoic	Tertiary	65 - 1.64
Mesozoic	Cretaceous	145 - 65
Mesozoic	Jurassic	208 - 145
Mesozoic	Triassic	245 - 208
Paleozoic	Permian	290 - 245
Paleozoic	Carboniferous	362 - 290
Paleozoic	Devonian	408 - 362
Paleozoic	Silurian	439 - 408
Paleozoic	Ordovician	510 - 439
Paleozoic	Cambrian	570 - 510

WHAT HAVE WE LEARNT FROM PREHISTORY?

Almost everything that we know about the living things on Earth before humans evolved has been learnt from fossils. Fossils are the remains of dead animals and plants that have been turned to stone over millions of years.

By studying these remains scientists have been able to come up with the type of animals that existed both on land and in water and also details of the type of food they needed to exist.

Records of prehistory and examples of fossils can be found in many of our modern museums.

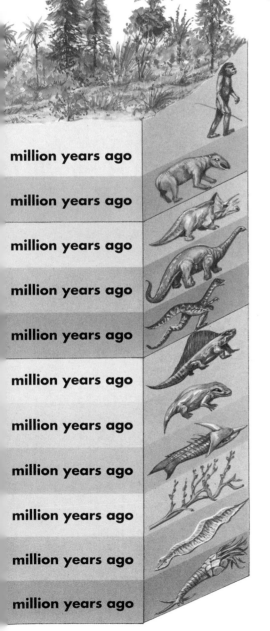

million years ago

million years ago

million years ago

million years ago

million years ago

million years ago

million years ago

million years ago

million years ago

million years ago

million years ago

million years ago

FACT FILE

This particular shark, called Carcharocles, lived about 15 million years ago, and was about the size of a bus. Only its huge teeth have survived and so scientists were only able to estimate its actual size.

When an organism dies, the soft parts rot away.

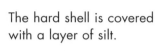

The hard shell is covered with a layer of silt.

A hard mineral fossil is gradually formed.

HOW ARE FOSSILS FORMED?

Fossils result from the death of an animal that took place millions of years ago. The soft parts of the animal rot quickly, and the bones or shell are scattered by scavenging animals.

Some of these remains are buried in mud or sand. If they are not disturbed in any way, more mud is deposited until the remains are deeply buried. Under great pressure from deposits above, the mud eventually compacts into sedimentary rock.

Sometimes a fossil will retain the shape and structure of the hard parts of an animal, such as fossilized dinosaur bones. These are not the original bones because minerals have replaced them over the years, but they retain the same shape. Other fossils are just the impression of an animal or plant created when it was buried.

FACT FILE

Trilobites were once among the most abundant animals on Earth. They lived only in the sea and survived for millions of years, evolving into some strangely shaped forms before they suddenly became extinct.

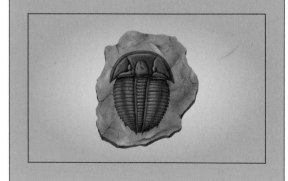

HOW ARE FOSSILS FOUND?

Every year fossils are found that add to our knowledge of prehistoric life. Very often they are discovered by ordinary people walking in the countryside. Places where soil is frequently being washed away from rocks, such as at the bottom of cliffs, are good places to look.

Fossils have been found accidentally by people working in mines or quarries. Sometimes they become exposed by erosion and can be seen sticking out of cliff faces.

Geologists are now able to identify those rock formations that are likely to contain fossils. More and more fossils are being found by properly organized expeditions.

Large numbers of new types of fossil are now being found in Mongolia and China. There, fossil hunters have unearthed what are probably the ancestors of modern birds. Palaeontology is the scientific name for the study of fossils.

FACT FILE

This skeleton of the early reptile Dimetrodon is unusually complete. Most fossil remains consist only of fragments, which must be pieced together.

HOW DID LIFE BEGIN ON LAND?

Plants were the first living things on our planet, starting with very simple plants such as algae. Then mosses and liverworts developed, followed by ferns and other larger plants. Animals did not leave the sea until plants had become fully established, otherwise there would have been no food for them.

Next were relatives of the spiders and scorpions, which were probably the first creatures to leave the sea and actually colonize on land. Later they evolved into larger and more complex forms of life. Amphibians multiplied rapidly, and the word actually means 'living on land and in water'.

FACT FILE

The first mammals lived alongside the dinosaurs, but in comparison with reptiles they were tiny and insignificant, like the Glyptodon below.

WHY DID SOME FISH BECOME LAND-DWELLERS?

Around 400 million years ago fish began to creep out of the water onto land. The main reasons for an animal to change its habits would be to obtain fresh food supplies and to escape from its predators. Many fish were able to just wriggle along on land, but in order to lift their body clear of the ground ordinary fins were not strong enough. One of these fish is the coelacanth, a large fish up to 3 ft (1 m) long with strange leg-like fins. It was found to contain bones that were very like those of land-living vertebrate animals. Relatives of the coelacanth had leg-like fins reinforced with bones, which allowed them to slither along like a modern crocodile. Many ancient fish developed simple lungs, which they used instead of their gills when they were out of the water.

FACT FILE

Baryonix is the only known fish-eating dinosaur, and uniquely it had huge claws on its front limbs.

HOW DO WE KNOW WHAT DINOSAURS WERE LIKE?

Although dinosaur remains are few, we know we can deduce quite a lot about them from their fossilized skeletons. We can calculate a dinosaur's weight by studying its bones. Heavy animals have massive bones to support their weight, while swift-moving hunters have very light, hollow bones. Muscles are firmly attached to bones, and although no trace of the muscles are left in the fossils, the points at which they attach can still be seen on the bones. These facts tell scientists how big the muscles must have been.

We know that a large digestive system is necessary to digest vegetable matter. The herbivores would have had massive barrel-shaped bodies, while carnivores would be slimmer. The shape of the teeth tells scientists what type of food the dinosaurs ate.

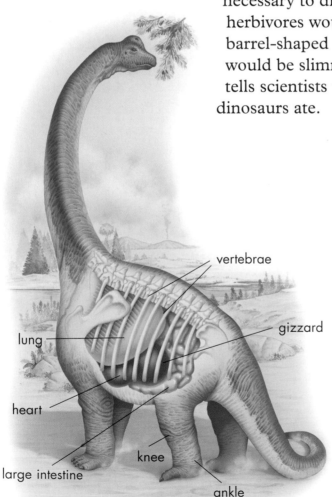

vertebrae

gizzard

lung

heart

large intestine

knee

ankle

FACT FILE

Much is presumed and guessed about dinosaurs. Looking at the Carnotaurus, it had weak jaws and was not well equipped for hunting, so it was assumed that it only fed on small prey.

HOW DID DINOSAURS EVOLVE?

Dinosaurs were reptiles that evolved into the most varied kinds of any living creature. They ranged from tiny bird-like animals to monstrous beasts that were the largest animals to ever live on land.

The dinosaurs survived for about 150 million years. They were not all meat-eating killers as often portrayed in books and films. Most dinosaurs were peaceful, browsing animals about the size of modern farm livestock.

The main thing that distinguishes dinosaurs from other reptiles is the way their body is supported by their legs. The legs of ancient and existing reptiles stick out sideways, so the body drags on the ground for most of the time. It is raised briefly when the animal runs. The skeletons of dinosaurs developed so the legs were beneath the body, raising the whole body off the ground.

FACT FILE

Some dinosaurs had characteristics the purposes of which are unknown, as in this Saurolophyus that had a large bony ridge on the top of its skull.

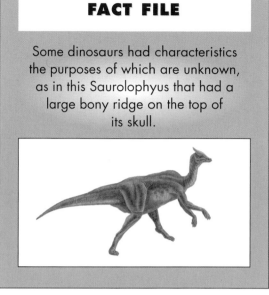

HOW MANY DIFFERENT TYPES OF DINOSAUR WERE THERE?

Pachycephalosaurus

There were thousands of different species of dinosaur and we have only discovered a small proportion of them. It is important at this stage to realise how rare fossils are. There were a few dinosaur species that must have been very common, like Iguanodon, which left many fossils. Others were probably scarce when they were alive, or lived in regions where fossilization was unlikely, and so there are few remains of these dinosaurs.

Herbivores often lived in groups or herds, but carnivores were usually more solitary and their fossils are therefore more rare. Many of the interesting dinosaurs are known from a single fossil, or one or two bones, and scientists must deduce the shape and size from these.

FACT FILE

Although in many ways the Ouranosaurus was a typical plant-eating dinosaur, it had a remarkable sail-like crest on its back and tail. Its function is not known.

How big were Dinosaurs?

Euoplocephalus

Dinosaurs vary in size enormously. Some were only about the size of a chicken, or even smaller. Compsognathus was only about 28 inches (70 cm) long and was very slightly built. It was an agile and fast-moving creature and is thought to have lived on insects and small animals. The skeleton of this dinosaur is very similar to that of a modern bird.

Scientists cannot agree on the maximum size of giant dinosaurs. But it is usually said that Brachiosaurus is the biggest, and is thought to have been about 100 ft (30 m) long and to have weighed as much as 128 tons (130 tonnes). This would make it by far the heaviest land animal to have ever existed. The Sauroposeidon has been described as being as high as 56 ft (17.2 m), making it three times the height of the tallest giraffe.

FACT FILE

The biggest mammal to have lived on Earth actually preceded dinosaurs. It was called the Indicotherium and was big enough to push over trees which were too tall for it to graze upon.

HOW DID CARNIVOROUS DINOSAURS CATCH THEIR PREY?

All meat-eating dinosaurs were roughly the same shape, but they all varied in size a great deal. They all belonged to a group called theropods meaning 'beast feet'.

The giant dinosaurs like Tyrannosaurus rex probably ambushed their prey, charging at them with jaws wide open. They could run at a speed of 32 mph (50 kph), although probably for only a very short distance. The impact of seven tonnes of dinosaur hitting its prey with a jagged mouthful of teeth would likely kill most animals outright.

Many smaller dinosaurs retained powerful front limbs and claws, and could cling to their prey while biting it.

FACT FILE

Plant-eating dinosaurs had long necks to enable them to reach trees, which were their main source of food.

Saltasaurus

Tyrannosaurus rex, usually just called T-rex, was the largest and most fearsome land-living predator ever to have existed.

Tyrannosaurus rex

HOW DID PLANT-EATING DINOSAURS FIND FOOD?

Hadrosaurus

Hadrosaurus was a large plant-eater that walked sometimes on two legs and at other times on four.

The type of food that plant-eating dinosaurs fed on depended on their type of mouth. Some had broad mouths like a duck's bill and they probably grazed on a mixture of plants. Dinosaurs with narrow jaws, most likely selected particular plants to eat.

The long-necked sauropods probably grazed on leaves and shoots. Large herds of sauropods would have caused tremendous devastation by feeding in this way and may have used their great weight to push trees over so they were easier to reach.

A herd of sauropods would have cleared great areas of trees, creating large expanses of open ground where smaller dinosaurs could graze. Dinosaurs with cutting beaks would have been able to crop the vegetation short.

FACT FILE

The diets of some dinosaurs are a complete mystery. For example, the Segnosaurus could have eaten termites, fish, or plants.

DID DINOSAURS LOOK AFTER THEIR YOUNG?

Very large numbers of remains of Protoceratops have been found in the Gobi desert, including eggs and nestlings. These animals seem to have nested in very large groups and probably cared for their young.

It was thought at one time that dinosaurs laid their eggs in isolated places. But in 1978 a remarkable find was made in Montana, USA. Fifteen Maiasaurus babies were found scattered around a large mound-shaped structure, together with many broken eggshells. The babies were not newly hatched because their teeth were partly worn away. The nest itself was about 7 ft (2 m) across and covered with vegetation.

FACT FILE

The eggs of Orodromeus have been found broken open from the inside as the young hatched out. The baby dinosaurs are thought to have foraged for their food while being guarded by adults.

In the Gobi desert, the pig-sized dinosaur Protoceratops dug holes in the sand and buried her eggs. She left them to hatch in the heat of the sand while she guarded them from predators. The eggs were arranged in careful circles, in layers. Presumably the mother dinosaur turned herself above the nest as she laid each egg.

HOW BIG WERE DINOSAUR EGGS?

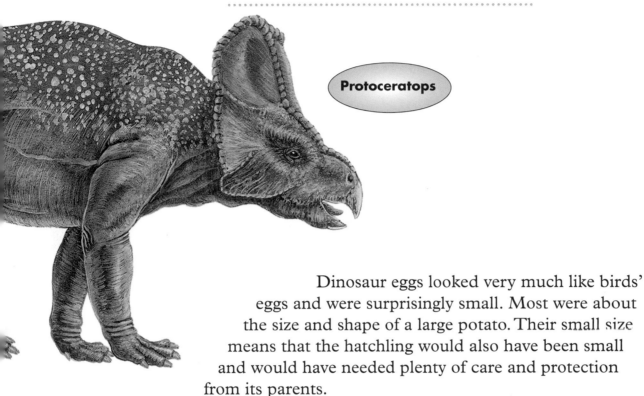

Protoceratops

Dinosaur eggs looked very much like birds' eggs and were surprisingly small. Most were about the size and shape of a large potato. Their small size means that the hatchling would also have been small and would have needed plenty of care and protection from its parents.

When Orodromeus nests were discovered, other dinosaur eggs were found between them. These eggs were smaller and were laid in straight lines. It has recently been found that they are the eggs of a small predator called the Troodon. It appears to have laid its eggs in the Orodromeus colony to gain protection from other predators. This habit is similar to that of modern cuckoos and their relatives, although they also use another species of bird to raise their young.

FACT FILE

The Oviraptor was an odd dinosaur that may have lived entirely on the eggs of other dinosaurs. It was bird-shaped, with a powerful beak for crushing eggs and did not have any teeth.

Euoplocephalus

HOW DID DINOSAURS PROTECT THEMSELVES?

Dinosaurs had various ways of protecting themselves. Firstly they might just have been too big to be brought down and eaten. Secondly, some dinosaurs could run very fast indeed, which meant they escaped their predator. Thirdly, a slow-moving dinosaur may have been covered with spikes and horns to help deter attackers.

FACT FILE

Although the sides of its body were less heavily armoured than many of its relatives, the underside of the Minmi was well protected by being covered with tough bony plates.

As well as being covered with jointed armour and defensive spines, the Euoplocephalus carried a massive club on the end of its tail, which would have crushed any predator.

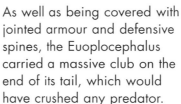

HOW DID DINOSAURS USE THEIR ARMOUR?

FACT FILE

Although some dinosaurs could not run very fast at all, they had other ways of defending themselves. The Shunasaurus had a tail club that it would wield in defence.

Several theories have been put forward as to why some dinosaurs had armour on parts of their body. The plates on the back of the Stegosaurus could have been used to display to rival animals, or perhaps help to regulate body temperature. It has even been suggested that the plates could have folded flat to make a sheet of armour over the animal's back. The whole head of an Ankylosaur was covered with protective plates and this cover even extended over the eyes. Others wielded their tails in defence.

HOW DID FISH EVOLVE?

Killer fish

As fish developed jaws, they were able to hunt other animals. Soon they evolved into large creatures, sometimes with armour to protect themselves. The most fearsome fish grew to 29 ft (9 m) in length.

Fossils show that the first fish occurred in the Ordovician Period which began about 460,000,000 years ago. These fish were jawless, and the most primitive of all. Their mouths were a simple opening, suited to feeding on the tiny animals that lay hidden in the mud.

Next came fish with jaws. Jaws allowed fish to explore various food sources and to feed more efficiently. Early fish with jaws are called placoderms. The jaws actually evolved from a set of gill arches that were present in the jawless fish. Gill arches are the bony supports of the gills.

From these placoderms came our present-day fish, the sharks and bony fish.

FACT FILE

Ammonites were relatives of the modern octopus and squid. They secreted a hard shell, living in a small compartment. A new compartment was added as they grew larger, eventually producing a spiral shell.

WHAT DID MARINE REPTILES LOOK LIKE?

The ichthyosaurs looked very much like modern dolphins, but were totally aquatic reptiles that gave birth to live young.

Mesosaurus was a small ancestor of the crocodile. Its remains have been found in both North and South America.

FACT FILE

Although looking at them you might think a crocodile is a dinosaur, you would be wrong. They both evolved from the same type of ancestors and crocodiles have changed very little over millions of years.

Many reptiles returned to the sea. Some of the most familiar ones are the plesiosaurs, large animals with a barrel-like body and a long snaky neck. They did not have a flexible body, they rowed themselves along by waving their fin-like front and rear limbs up and down.

Pliosaurs were relatives of the plesiosaurs but had shorter necks and massive skulls armed with enormous teeth. They were the largest and most powerful predators ever known.

Turtles also developed at about the same time. Unlike modern ones, the early forms did not have a complete shell.

WHAT SIZE WERE PTEROSAURS?

Various reptiles have developed the ability to glide, but the pterosaurs were the only ones to develop true flight. Their arms were quite short and their wings were supported by an enormously long fourth finger, leaving the other fingers free to function as a hand. A thin, skin-like membrane was stretched from the elongated finger to the sides of the body, and sometimes to the hind legs.

The whole body was extremely light with hollow bones. Many pterosaurs lived a similar life to the modern seagull and albatross. One pterosaur discovered, the Quetzalcoatlus, had a wing span greater than 48 ft (15 m) which is larger than that of many light planes.

FACT FILE

The Pterodactylus was a very small flying reptile, smaller than a modern pigeon and much lighter in build. It had a wing span of 40cm across, which means it would have been a fast and agile flyer.

Scientists were astounded when the remains of Quetzalcoatlus were found. It proved to be the largest flying creature ever to have existed.

HOW DID PTEROSAURS FLY?

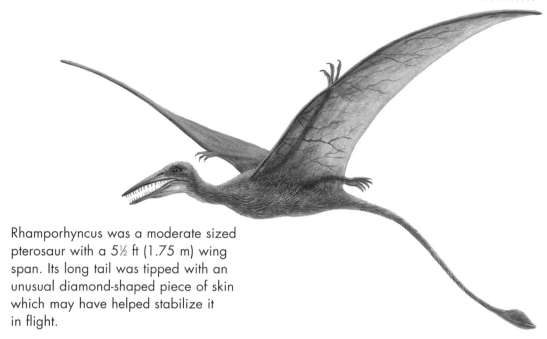

Rhamporhyncus was a moderate sized pterosaur with a 5½ ft (1.75 m) wing span. Its long tail was tipped with an unusual diamond-shaped piece of skin which may have helped stabilize it in flight.

It was believed at one time that the pterosaurs were unable to flap their wings and fly like a bird. They probably launched themselves off cliffs and glided on upward currents of air.

More recently, however, it has been suggested that pterosaurs were actually very efficient flyers. Some of the smallest types would not have been very effective gliders and must have fluttered their wings like modern birds. This would not have been possible for the giant pterosaurs, which must have been pure gliders.

Pterosaurs did not have feathers, because their large wings were more like those of a bat than a bird. However, pterosaurs did have fur! This seems to suggest that they were warm-blooded, as there would be no point in the body of a cold-blooded creature, such as a modern reptile, being insulated.

FACT FILE

The small predatory therapod dinosaur Campsognathus resembles Archaeopteryx so closely that the remains of the two animals have sometimes been confused. This seems to prove the dinosaur ancestry to birds.

WHY DID THE DINOSAURS DIE OUT?

Dinosaurs lived for a long time – some 150 million years – before they died out about 65 million years ago. During their time on the Earth they dominated the land, while other reptile relatives dominated the sea and the air. Before the dinosaurs disappeared completely there were two mass extinctions when a large number of species died out. The dinosaurs survived, however, until the end of the Cretaceous Period.

Many people believe that dinosaurs became extinct as a result of climate change after a huge meteor or a small asteroid struck the Earth.

The other theory is that it coincided with a period of high volcanic activity, which could have wiped out the whole population. However, it was not only the dinosaurs that became extinct. At the same time most marine reptiles and pterosaurs also died out as did tiny plankton whose shells form chalk deposits, ammonites and the remaining species of trilobites. It is difficult to imagine the exact causes of this extinction. For instance, how did turtles manage to survive?

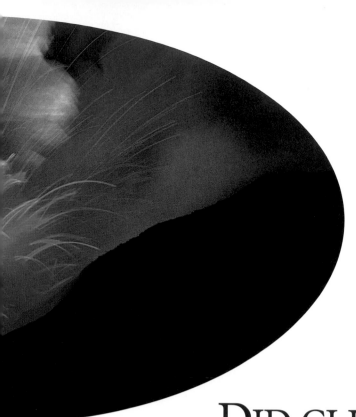

High volcanic activity could have contributed to the dinosaurs' extinction.

DID CLIMATE AFFECT THE DINOSAURS' SURVIVAL?

During the late Cretaceous Period the world's continents were drifting into new positions. This constant shifting within the crust led to a huge increase in volcanic activity. Volcanoes spewed out hot lava and gases, which could have built up in the atmosphere to such high levels that they affected dinosaurs and their plant food.

Other climatic changes like an ice age may have wiped out many species of dinosaur that were unable to adapt to the extreme cold.

FACT FILE

The Earth went through some incredible climate changes during the era of the dinosaurs and one of the theories regarding their extinction would have been an extreme ice age. There are very few plants or animals that could have survived this extreme cold.

HOW DID MAMMALS EVOLVE?

A group of mammal-like reptiles preceded the appearance of the dinosaurs. These early mammals gradually disappeared, however, during the Triassic Period and were replaced by the true mammals.

It is hard to decide exactly which of these extinct animals was a reptile and which was a mammal. It is quite probable that the later reptiles had hair and other mammal-like characteristics. The first mammals were small and were vulnerable to all the fierce dinosaur predators. Once the dinosaurs died out the mammals were able to develop properly and evolve. Eventually the mammals grew into forms that were almost as gigantic as their dinosaur predecessors.

Thylacosmilus

Thylacosmilus was a typical example of the sabre-tooth cats, with long canine teeth that were used to stab its prey.

FACT FILE

Mammoths closely resembled modern elephants but were covered with thick, coarse hair and were adapted to live in the cold tundra regions. They survived in northern Arctic regions until well after the appearance of man, who hunted them to extinction.

ARE MARSUPIALS SIMILAR TO THE FIRST MAMMALS?

It is said that marsupials, like the kangaroo, are actually primitive mammals because they give birth to tiny, undeveloped young. The young are raised in a pouch until they are developed enough to live on their own. There are two kinds of mammal, however, that still lay eggs like their reptile ancestors. Both the duck-billed platypus and the spiny anteater, or echidna, live in Australia. They lay eggs and the hatchlings are placed in a pouch on their mother's stomach. Unlike the young of reptiles, these babies are nourished by their mother's milk. These two very unusual animals give us some indication about how the earliest mammals may have developed.

FACT FILE

Also known as Zeuglodon, Basilosaurus is the most commonly found of the ancient fossil whales. It was a predator like modern dolphins. When whales die their remains usually sink in deep water where they are unlikely to form fossils.

The Human Body

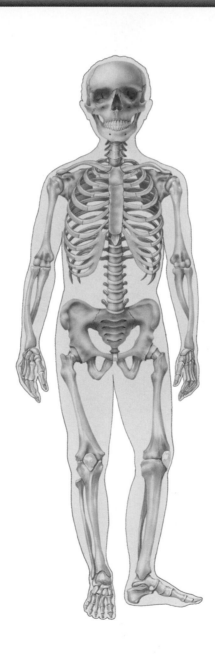

Bones & Muscles

WHICH BONES FORM THE PELVIS? 116
HOW MANY MUSCLES ARE THERE IN THE HUMAN BODY? 117

WHERE ARE THE SMOOTH MUSCLES FOUND? 118
WHAT IS BONE MADE FROM? 119

HOW DO MUSCLES WORK? 120
HOW DO JOINTS WORK? 121

HOW CAN MUSCLES WORK IN PAIRS? 122
HOW DO MUSCLES RESPOND TO ACTIVITY? 123

HOW DOES A BROKEN BONE HEAL? 124
HOW DO CUTS AND GRAZES HEAL THEMSELVES? 125

WHERE IS THE SMALLEST BONE IN YOUR BODY? 126
WHERE ARE THE VERTEBRAE? 127

WHERE IS THE LARGEST JOINT IN THE BODY? 128
WHERE IS THE LARGEST MUSCLE IN THE BODY? 129

WHY IS EXERCISE GOOD FOR US? 130
WHY DO MUSCLES ACHE AFTER EXERCISE? 131

WHY DO WE HAVE A SKELETON? 132

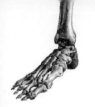

WHICH BONES FORM THE PELVIS?

The pelvis is formed by two large symmetrical hip bones, which are joined in front as the pubic symphysis. In the back, they are attached firmly to the sacrum. In adults, each hip bone appears to be one solid bone, but in fact consists of three bones, the ilium, ischium, and pubis, that bind together as the body grows. When you put your hand on your hip, the broad, flat bone you can feel is the ilium; sitting down, your weight rests on the ischium.

Supporting the lower abdomen, the pelvis is a bony structure surrounding the urinary bladder, the last portion of the large intestine, and also, in females, the reproductive organs – hence a woman's pelvis is broader and flatter than a man's, with a larger central cavity.

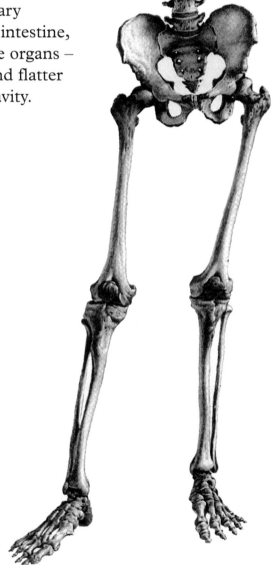

FACT FILE

The pelvis is joined to the spinal column at the sacroiliac joints. The lower part of the pelvis connects wth the thigh bones, or femurs, via ball-and-socket hip joints, enabling the legs to move in various positions.

Ball-and-socket joint

HOW MANY MUSCLES ARE THERE IN THE HUMAN BODY?

There are over 600 major muscles in the human body, or which about 240 have particular names. These muscles are divided into two main types, skeletal muscles and smooth muscles. A third type, which shares characteristics with skeletal and smooth muscles, and is only to be found in the heart, is called a cardiac muscle.

Holding the bones of the skeleton together, skeletal muscles enable the body to move as well as giving it its shape, and they form a large part of our face, neck, abdomen, arms and legs. The larger the job, the larger the muscle is generally the rule, so thcy can vary in size from the thigh muscles that have to be big and strong to the eye muscles that are small and fairly weak.

FACT FILE

Cardiac muscle makes up the walls of the heart. When cardiac muscle cells contract, they push blood out of the heart and into the arteries.

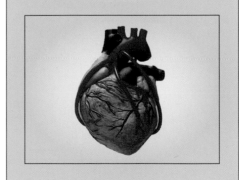

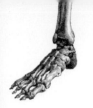

WHERE ARE THE SMOOTH MUSCLES FOUND?

The smooth muscles work slowly and automatically in a natural, rhythmic way, contracting then relaxing, controlling our many body processes. For example, the steady action of these muscles in the stomach and intestines moves food along for digestion. Smooth muscles are to be found in the walls of the stomach, intestines, blood vessels and bladder, and because they are not consciously controlled by the brain, we also know them as involuntary muscles. They react instead to stimulus from particular nerves that are part of the autonomic nervous system, and also to the effect of certain body chemicals.

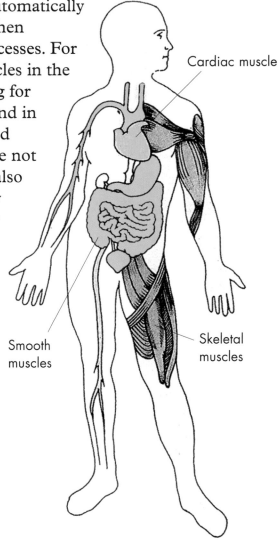

Cardiac muscle

Smooth muscles

Skeletal muscles

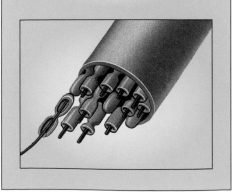

FACT FILE

Muscle cells are excitable because the membrane of each cell is electrically charged. Thus, a muscle cell is said to have electric potential.

WHAT IS BONE MADE FROM?

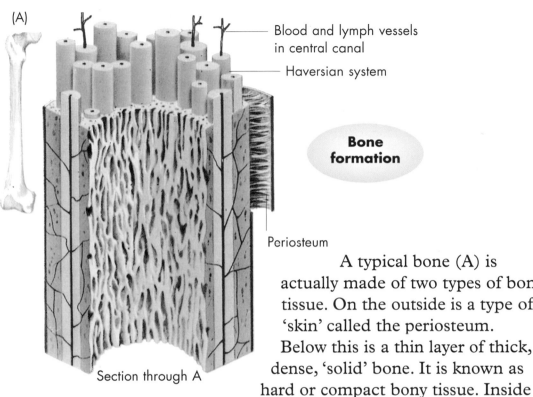

(A)

Blood and lymph vessels in central canal

Haversian system

Bone formation

Periosteum

Section through A

A typical bone (A) is actually made of two types of bony tissue. On the outside is a type of 'skin' called the periosteum.

Below this is a thin layer of thick, dense, 'solid' bone. It is known as hard or compact bony tissue. Inside this, and forming the bulk of the middle of the bone, is a different bony tissue, more like a sponge or honeycomb. It has gaps and spaces, and it is called spongy, or alveolar, bony tissue. It is much lighter than the outer compact bone, and the spaces are filled with blood vessels, and jelly-like bone marrow for making new blood cells.

FACT FILE

There are 206 bones in the average body. However, there are a few people who have more, such as an extra pair of ribs, making 13 pairs instead of 12 and therefore 208 bones in total.

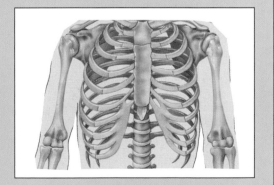

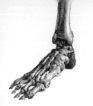

HOW DO MUSCLES WORK?

There are 639 muscles in the human body, each comprising around ten million muscle cells. Each of these cells is like a motor containing ten cylinders arranged in a row. The cylinders are tiny boxes that contain fluid and when a muscle contracts the brain sends a message to these tiny boxes. For a fraction of a second, the fluid in the tiny box congeals; then it becomes fluid again. It is this action that causes the muscle to move. When a muscle is stimulated into action, it reacts quickly – it may contract in less than one tenth of a second. But before it has time to relax, another message comes along. It contracts again and again. All these contractions take place so quickly that they become fused into one action with the result that the muscle performs one smooth, continuous action.

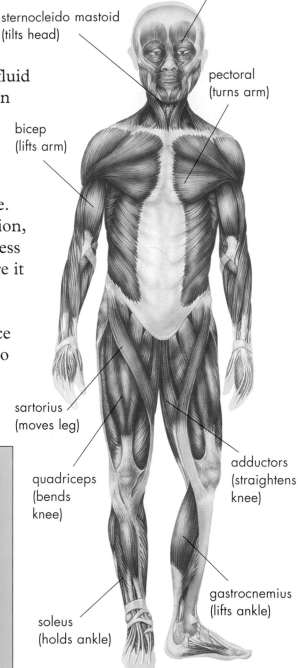

orbicularis oculi
(narrows eye)

sternocleido mastoid
(tilts head)

pectoral
(turns arm)

bicep
(lifts arm)

sartorius
(moves leg)

adductors
(straightens knee)

quadriceps
(bends knee)

gastrocnemius
(lifts ankle)

soleus
(holds ankle)

FACT FILE

When two muscles work against each other, they are always slightly contracted. This is called muscle tone. Active people tend to have better muscle tone.

HOW DO JOINTS WORK?

The human body has more than 100 joints. Some joints move like a simple hinge, such as those in the elbows and knees. Other joints move in all directions, such as the shoulder joint or the base of the thumb. Joints in the spine allow only a small amount of movement. The ends of most bones are covered with tough rubbery cartilage, which cushions them from impact as we move. Many joints are lubricated with an oily liquid called synovial fluid so they can bend freely. Synovial fluid is held in a bladder between the layers of cartilage on the ends of the bone. These lubricated joints can move freely and without friction.

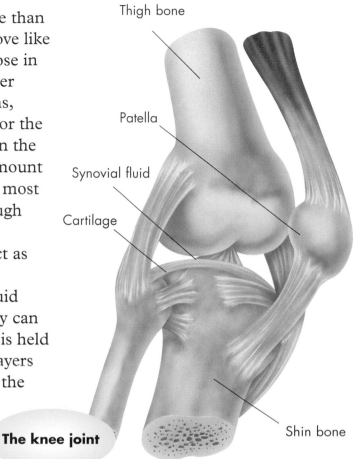

Thigh bone

Patella

Synovial fluid

Cartilage

Shin bone

The knee joint

FACT FILE

Regular exercise improves muscle strength and endurance, and keeps the body supple. It can also improve your body shape and posture as well as strengthening your heart and improving your blood flow. It will generally make you feel much better and help you to sleep soundly.

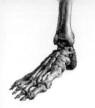

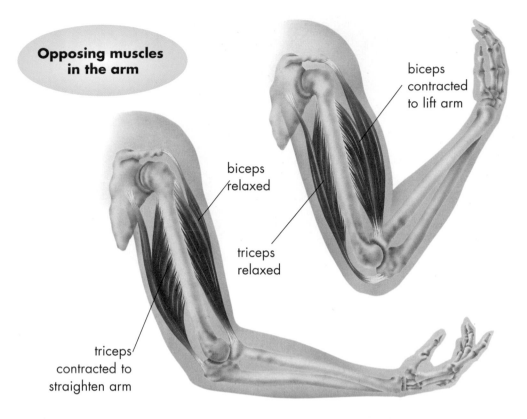

Opposing muscles in the arm

biceps
contracted
to lift arm

biceps
relaxed

triceps
relaxed

triceps
contracted to
straighten arm

HOW CAN MUSCLES WORK IN PAIRS?

Muscles actually work in pairs. A muscle can only pull in one direction so it needs another muscle to pull in the opposite direction in order to return a bone to its original position. When you lift your forearm, the biceps muscle shortens to lift the bone. When you straighten your arm, the triceps muscle pulls it back again and the biceps relaxes. The same action takes place in your legs when you walk and run, and when you move your fingers and toes.

FACT FILE

Metabolism is the sum of all chemical activity in our cells which break down the food we take in. Our metabolic rate increases with exercise, which means that we use the energy we get from food much more efficiently.

HOW DO MUSCLES RESPOND TO ACTIVITY?

Muscles are made up of long, thin cells called muscle fibres. But muscles differ in what they do and how they do it. When a muscle contracts, it produces an acid known as lactic acid. This acid is like a poison, with the effect of making you feel tired, by making the muscles feel tired. If the lactic acid is removed from a tired muscle, it stops feeling tired and you can go right to work again!

But, of course, lactic acid is not removed normally when you exercise and various toxins are produced when muscles are active. They are carried by the blood through the body and cause tiredness throughout the entire body, especially in the brain. So feeling tired after exercise is really the result of a kind of internal poisoning. However, the body needs this feeling of tiredness so that it will want to rest. During rest, waste products are removed, the cells recuperate, nerve cells of the brain recharge their batteries and the joints replace their supplies of lubricant they have used up. So while exercise is good for the body and muscles – rest is just as important!

FACT FILE

The knee is a typical load-bearing joint. The ends of the bone are cushioned by a pad of cartilage to protect them from impact. Wear and tear is minimized by a lubricant called synovial fluid.

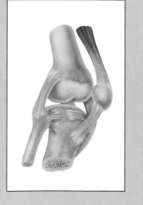

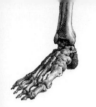

HOW DOES A BROKEN BONE HEAL?

When mending a broken bone, we – or our doctors – are helped in amazing ways by the body itself. The core to this is bone tissue, produced by the connective tissue cells in the broken bone. When a bone is broken, bone and tissue around the break are also damaged and some of this tissue dies. The entire area around the bone ends and tissue is held together by a combination of lymph and clotted blood.

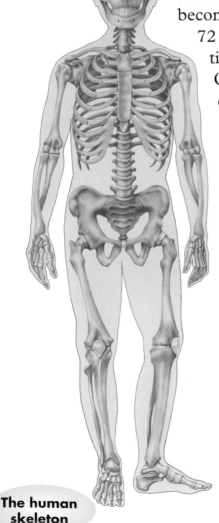

The human skeleton

The first stage in repairing a break comes after a few hours, when young new tissue cells start to appear. The cells multiply very quickly, becoming filled with calcium, and in between 72 to 96 hours after the fracture, they form a tissue which bonds the ends of the bones. Over the next few months normal bone develops, after the calcium which has been deposited in the newly formed tissue helps form hard bone. This is why, to keep the edges of the break in strict alignment by not allowing the bone to move while this process is taking place, a plaster cast is put on a broken limb.

FACT FILE

Constant use helps to keep the bones strong. Lack of exercise is one of the main reasons why elderly people's bones can become so weak and prone to easy breakage.

blood escapes   begins to clot   scab forms

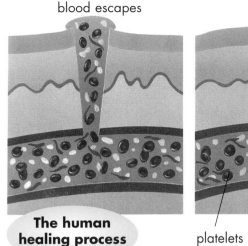
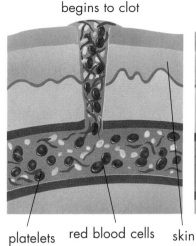
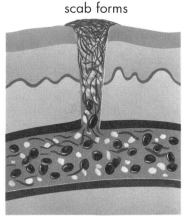

The human healing process

platelets   red blood cells   skin

HOW DO CUTS AND GRAZES HEAL THEMSELVES?

When we cut or graze ourselves, the body is able to heal itself. When the skin incurs a wound, platelets in the blood congregate at the site of the wound to form a temporary clot. This usually happens as soon as a wound is exposed to the air. This quickly plugs the wound.

White blood cells gather around the wound site to kill invading microbes, helping to prevent infection. New cells eventually grow into the wound replacing the damaged tissue. For a small cut or graze, this usually takes a couple of days. Soon the clotted material, which has formed a scab, falls off to reveal clean, new skin underneath. Sometimes we protect our grazes and cuts with plasters whilst our bodies deal with the repair.

FACT FILE

Cells need food, oxygen and water to survive. Food and water are supplied by blood and other body fluids, which also carry away wastes. Blood also contains food and chemicals needed by the cell.

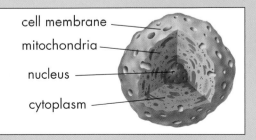

cell membrane

mitochondria

nucleus

cytoplasm

125

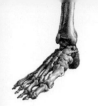

WHERE IS THE SMALLEST BONE IN YOUR BODY?

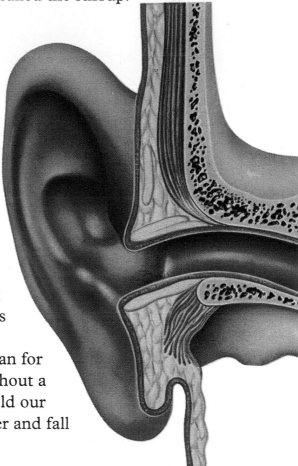

The smallest bone in the body is called the stirrup. It is in the middle ear and is part of the system that carries sound signals to the brain. At only 3mm long, the stirrup is about the size of a grain of rice. The footplate of the stirrup bone is attached to a membrane called the oval window, which leads to the inner ear. It is connected to two other very small bones called the hammer and anvil. All three of these bones are joined to the eardrum, where sound is collected before it is sent in the form of nerve signals to the brain.

The ear is a very important organ for keeping our sense of balance. Without a sense of balance, we could not hold our body steady, and we would stagger and fall when we tried to move.

FACT FILE

Some people suffer from motion sickness when they travel by boat, car, train, or airplane. Motion sickness is caused by excessive stimulation of the vestibular organs. But researchers do not know why some people develop motion sickness more easily than others do.

WHERE ARE THE VERTEBRAE?

The spine, which is also known as the spinal column, vertebral column, or backbone, is that part of the skeleton that extends down the middle of the back, and is made up of a column of bones called vertebrae. It plays a crucial part in our posture and movement, and also protects the all-important spinal cord.

Although some grow together later in life, the human spine basically consists of 33 vertebrae. There are 7 cervical (neck), 12 thoracic (chest region), 5 lumbar (lower back), 5 sacral (hip region), and 4 coccygeal (tailbone region) vertebrae. They are secured in place by a combination of muscles and strong connective tissue called ligaments. Most have fibrous intervertebral disks between them in order to absorb shock and enable the spine, which normally has a slight natural curve, to bend.

FACT FILE

Many people suffer from backaches. Sometimes the intervertebral disk, the tissue that lies between the vertebrae, sticks out and presses on nerves. This condition is called a slipped disk. It can cause severe pain in the lower back, thighs, and legs.

Cross-section of the spinal column

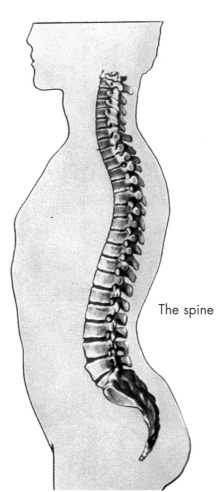

The spine

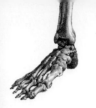

WHERE IS THE LARGEST JOINT IN THE BODY?

The knee joint is the largest and most complex joint in the body. The knee is the joint where the thighbone meets the large bone of the lower leg. The knee moves like a hinge, but it can also rotate and move a little from side to side. The knee is more likely to be damaged than most other joints because it is subject to tremendous forces during vigorous activity. Most of the knee injuries that occur in football and other sports result from twisting the joint. The knee ligaments are the strongest connections between the femur and the tibia. Ligaments keep the bones from moving out of position.

Patella

Tibia

Fibula

FACT FILE

The patella (or kneecap) is a small, flat, triangular bone in front of the joint. It is not directly connected with any other bone. Muscle attachments hold it in place.

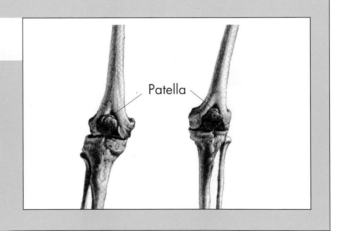

Patella

WHERE IS THE LARGEST MUSCLE IN THE BODY?

The largest muscle in the human body is called the gluteus maximus and this is situated in the buttocks, while the smallest is the stapedius which can be found in the middle ear. A muscle is the tough, elastic tissue that makes body parts move. Muscles are found throughout the body. As a person grows, the muscles also get bigger. Muscle makes up nearly half the body weight of an adult.

Of over 600 muscles in the human body, no less than 240 have specific names. They fall into two main categories, skeletal muscles and smooth muscles, while a third type, called cardiac muscle and only to be found in the heart, has similarities to both the skeletal and smooth muscles. People use muscles to make various movements.

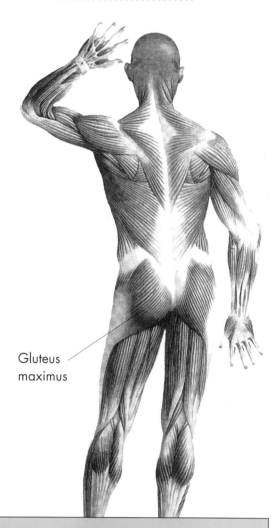

Gluteus maximus

FACT FILE

The longest muscle is the sartorius, which runs from the side of the waist, diagonally down across the front of the thigh to the inside of the knee. Among the most powerful muscles are the masseters, one on each side of the face.

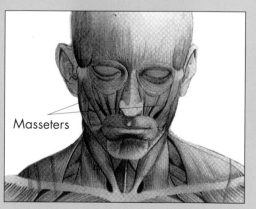

Masseters

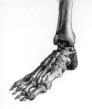

WHY IS EXERCISE GOOD FOR US?

Regular exercise is important because it keeps bones, joints and muscles healthy. During any physical exertion, the rate at which the heart beats increases, as it pumps more oxygenated blood around the body. How quickly the heart rate returns to normal after exercise is one way to assess how fit someone is and how exercise is actually improving their fitness.

Once almost everyone did manual work of some kind. It was essential for survival. Human bodies were not designed for the inactive lives many of us now lead. That is why exercise is important for good health.

FACT FILE

Swimming is a very good form of exercise as it uses lots of muscles without causing strain.

WHY DO MUSCLES ACHE AFTER EXERCISE?

FACT FILE

It is important to stretch your muscles before and after exercise to distribute the lactic acid.

After any kind of exercise the muscles will contract, and in doing so produce an acid called lactic acid. Acting almost like a 'poison', the immediate effect will be to make the individual tired by having a 'tiring' effect on the muscles. Once this acid disappears from a muscle, it stops feeling tired and can function normally.

But this type of body 'poisoning' serves a purpose in that by making a person tired they will want to rest, and it's during periods of rest that the joints of the body are able to replace the necessary lubricants that have been used up.

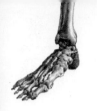

WHY DO WE HAVE A SKELETON?

A skeleton is made up of a network of bones. Bones provide a framework that holds the whole body together.

Without a skeleton we would not be supported and would simply flop about like a rag doll. This would mean that we would not be able to move about.

The skeleton also gives protection to delicate organs in our bodies such as the brain, heart and lungs. It acts as a support to all the soft parts of the body. The skeleton also provides a system of levers that the muscles can work on, enabling us to carry out all our movements.

FACT FILE

At birth a baby has 300 bones, but 94 join together in early childhood. Your hand and wrist alone contain 27 bones.

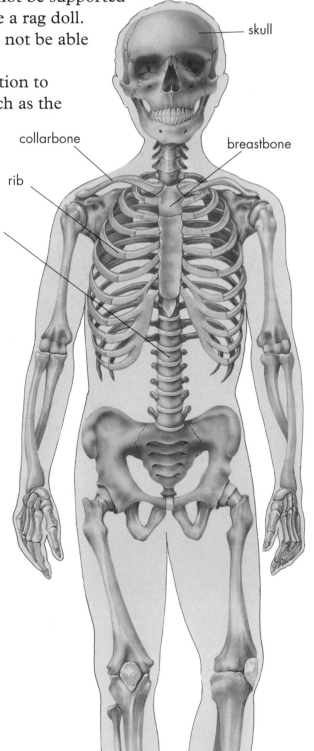

skull

collarbone

breastbone

rib

backbone

132

Heart & Circulation

WHERE IS OUR CIRCULATORY SYSTEM? 134
WHERE ARE THE AORTIC AND PULMONIC VALVES? 135

WHY DOESN'T BLOOD FLOW BACKWARDS? 136
WHERE ARE THE JUGULAR VEINS SITUATED? 137

HOW DOES THE HEART WORK? 138
WHAT IS BLOOD MADE FROM? 139

WHAT IS BLOOD CLOTTING? 140
WHAT IS LYMPH? 141

WHEN DO PEOPLE GET HEART ATTACKS? 142
WHEN DOES THE HEART STOP BEATING? 143

WHEN DOES BLOOD FLOW FROM VEINS TO ARTERIES? 144
WHEN DO RED AND WHITE BLOOD CELLS DIE? 145

WHEN ARE OUR BLOOD GROUPS DETERMINED? 146

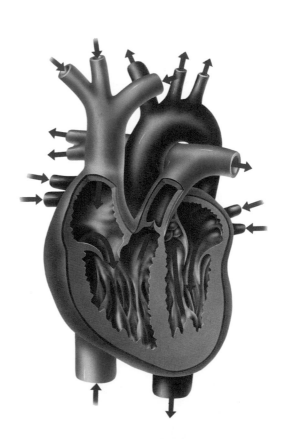

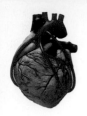

WHERE IS OUR CIRCULATORY SYSTEM?

Heart

Arteries (red)

Veins (blue)

The aortic and pulmonic valves are in the heart. The network that carries blood throughout the body is an amazing natural device known as the circulatory system. Not only does it supply the cells of the body with the food and oxygen they need to survive, it carries carbon dioxide and other waste matter away from the cells, helps regulate the body's temperature and transports elements that protect the body from disease. The network also allows the movement of chemical substances called hormones, which help regulate and stabilize the functioning of various parts of the body. The blood vessels, which form a complex system of connecting tubes throughout the body, fall into three major categories. The arteries transport blood from the heart, the veins return the blood back to the heart, while the capillaries are minute vessels that connect the arteries and the veins.

FACT FILE

The three main parts of the human circulatory system are the heart, the blood vessels, and the blood. In addition a watery fluid called lymph, and the vessels that carry it, are often thought of as part of the circulatory system.

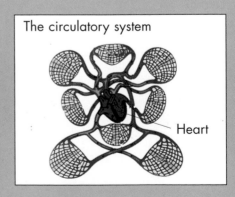

The circulatory system

Heart

WHERE ARE THE AORTIC AND PULMONIC VALVES?

The heart pumps blood on both sides at the same time. The right ventricle contracts, sending blood to the lungs, while the left ventricle contracts and squeezes blood out to the body. There are two stages in the heart's cycle of activity, called systole and diastole. The systole stage happens when the ventricles contract, and the diastole stage occurs when the ventricles relax and the atria contract. One full cycle of contraction and relaxation makes a heartbeat, and is known as the cardiac cycle. During every cardiac cycle, the heart valves open and close, and it's the closing of the valves that makes the pulsing sound of a heartbeat, which doctors listen to with a stethoscope. With the ventricles' contraction the mitral and tricuspid valves close, creating the first sound ①. As soon as the valves close, pressure in the ventricles forces the aortic and pulmonic valves to open ②. After a contraction ends, the ventricle pressure drops ③, the aortic and pulmonic valves closing and causing most of the second heart sound ④.

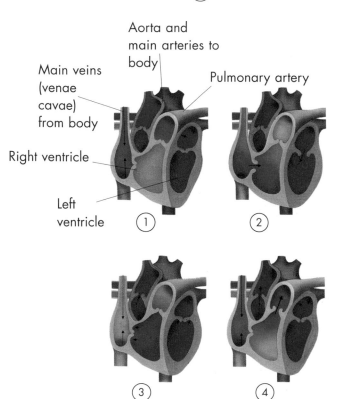

Aorta and main arteries to body

Main veins (venae cavae) from body

Pulmonary artery

Right ventricle

Left ventricle

① ② ③ ④

FACT FILE

The heart of an average person at rest beats 60 to 80 times each minute. Each beat sends about $2\frac{1}{2}$ ounces of blood out of each ventricle. This means that, at rest, the heart pumps some $2\frac{1}{2}$ gallons of blood each minute.

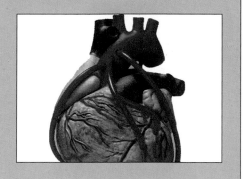

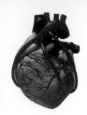

WHY DOESN'T BLOOD FLOW BACKWARDS?

Blood is transported to the heart by means of blood vessels called veins, part of the whole system of blood vessels via which blood circulates. The blood in your veins travels quite slowly, and many large veins have valves to stop the blood from draining backwards towards the legs and feet.

Blood flowing forwards forces the valve flaps to open ①. Blood flowing back forces them to shut ②. The valves in the heart work in exactly the same way.

Blood is also helped along by the arm and leg muscles contracting. That is why, if you stand still for a long period of time, blood can collect in your legs and make them puffy and sore.

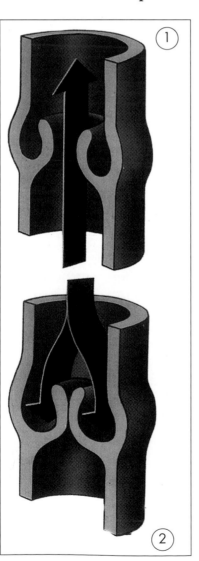

FACT FILE

The lymphatic system is one of the body's defences against infection. Harmful particles and bacteria that have entered the body are filtered out by small masses of tissue that lie along the lymphatic vessels. These bean-shaped masses are called lymph nodes.

WHERE ARE THE JUGULAR VEINS SITUATED?

There are four large veins that return blood to the heart from the head and neck, called jugular veins. They get their name from the Latin word for collarbone, jugulus. The jugular veins are situted on either side of the neck, each side having an external and internal jugular. The external jugulars carry blood from external parts of the head and neck to the heart and are close to the surface, while the internal jugulars lie deeper, with blood from the deeper neck tissues of the neck and the interior of the skull. 'Going for the jugular' is a well-known phrase, referring to opening the much larger internal jugular vein, which usually proves fatal, because of the rapid loss of blood that invariably occurs.

FACT FILE

Whiplash is a term commonly used to describe a type of injury to the neck. This kind of injury results from a sudden blow that throws the head rapidly backward and forward.

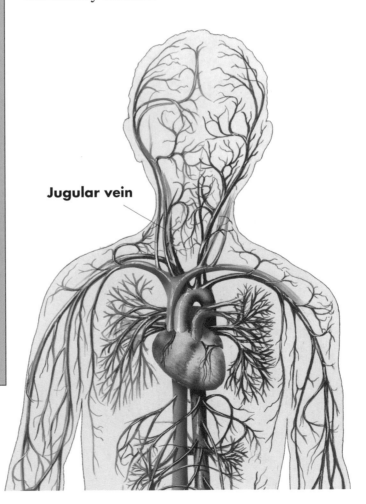

Jugular vein

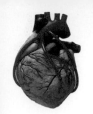

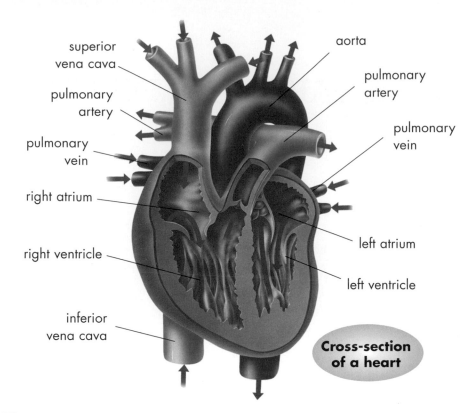

superior
vena cava

aorta

pulmonary
artery

pulmonary
artery

pulmonary
vein

pulmonary
vein

right atrium

left atrium

right ventricle

left ventricle

inferior
vena cava

**Cross-section
of a heart**

HOW DOES THE HEART WORK?

The heart is a fist-sized muscular organ that pumps blood around the body. It is actually two pumps that are joined together. At the top of each side of the heart is a thin-walled chamber called the atrium which receives blood that returns to the heart through the veins. Once the atrium is filled, it contracts and squeezes its blood into a much more muscular chamber called the ventricle. The ventricle contracts in turn and forces blood at high pressure along the arteries and off to the lungs or the rest of the body. A system of one way valves stops the blood from leaking back into the heart. The left side of the heart pumps blood to the lungs to collect more oxygen.

FACT FILE

An electrocardiogram, or ECG, measures the electrical signals that the heart produces as it beats. These signals change when a person suffers from certain medical conditions that affect the heart. They are measured by attaching wires to the chest near the heart. A doctor can study results as printed information.

WHAT IS BLOOD MADE FROM?

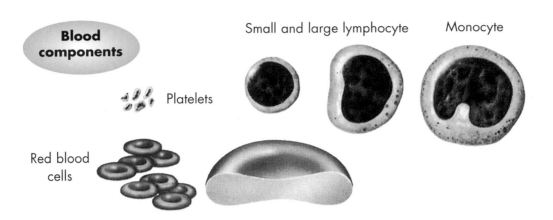

Blood components

Small and large lymphocyte

Monocyte

Platelets

Red blood cells

Blood is the fluid that is pumped around the body in the circulatory system. Blood carries oxygen, which it picks up in the lungs. It distributes this oxygen to all body parts, since every body cell needs a regular supply of oxygen to stay alive. Blood is made up of many components and has many functions. It consists of a yellow fluid, called plasma, in which red and white blood corpuscles and platelets are suspended. The capillaries allow fluid to escape from the blood. The cells and large proteins are left in the vessel and this fluid can now become the interstitial fluid (a background fluid that acts as an active support). This will either return to the capillary or join the lymphatic system. Blood amounts to about one-third of the total interstitial fluid.

The red and white blood cells are formed in the bone marrow. The plasma occupies about 55 percent of the blood volume. It is 90 percent water, 7 percent proteins, with the remaining 3 percent made up of small molecules.

FACT FILE

Blood is warm and works like the liquid in a central heating system. It absorbs warmth from the busy parts such as the heart and muscles and spreads it out to cooler parts like the skin.

Plasma

White blood cells

Red blood cells

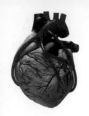

WHAT IS BLOOD CLOTTING?

When you cut yourself, the blood clots to prevent the wound from bleeding. Clotting is caused by substances in the blood. Together with small particles called platelets, these substances produce masses of fine mesh when they are exposed to air. They block the wound and prevent more blood loss. New cells grow rapidly into the wound, replacing the damaged tissue. Soon the clotted material, called a scab, falls off and clean, new skin is revealed underneath.

FACT FILE

Your blood pressure can be measured by a doctor with a special blood pressure monitor. During sleep your blood pressure decreases slightly, and during exercise and emotional excitement it increases.

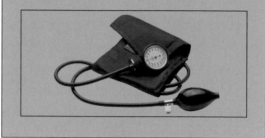

Tissue factor

Fibrinogen

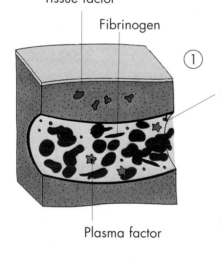

①

Platelet

Plasma factor

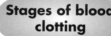

Stages of blood clotting

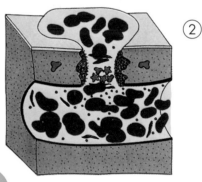

③

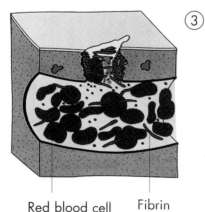

Red blood cell   Fibrin

②

④

WHAT IS LYMPH?

Your body's main attack force is called the lymph system. Like the blood system, it is a set of vessels which carry liquid round the body. This liquid is called lymph. Lymph contains special white blood cells called lymphocytes. These can make substances called antibodies which fight germs and cope with poisons. It works in the following way: The fluid passes out of the capillary ① and either into the vein or into the smallest, thin-walled lymph vessel ②. These vessels join together to form large channels and finally reach the thoracic duct running next to the descending aorta. This duct joins one of the main branches of the superior vena cava ⑤. Valves ③ keep lymph flowing in one direction. Lymph glands ④ are found throughout the body and at places where lymph vessels unite ⑥.

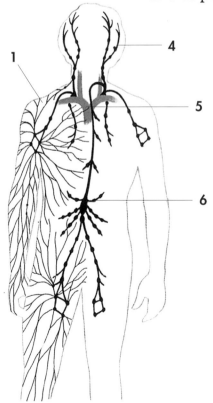

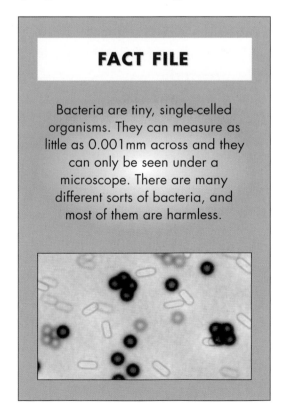

FACT FILE

Bacteria are tiny, single-celled organisms. They can measure as little as 0.001mm across and they can only be seen under a microscope. There are many different sorts of bacteria, and most of them are harmless.

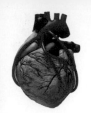

WHEN DO PEOPLE GET HEART ATTACKS?

Your heart is a powerful muscle which pumps blood around your body. It is only the size of your fist and weighs less than half a kilogram. Each and every day it pumps about 18,000 litres of blood around your body, and yet you are not normally aware that it is even beating. Run quickly upstairs, though, and you will soon feel it thumping away inside your rib cage.

A heart attack can occur when the inability of either or both sides of the heart to pump sufficient blood to meet the needs of our body. Other prominent causes of a heart attack are abnormally high blood pressure (hypertension), coronary atherosclerosis (the presence of fatty deposits in the lining of the coronary arteries), and rheumatic heart disease.

A person with left-sided heart failure experiences shortness of breath after exertion, difficulty in breathing while lying down, spasms of breathlessness at night, and abnormally high pressure in the pulmonary veins. A person with right-sided failure experiences abnormally high pressure in the systemic veins, enlargement of the liver, and accumulation of fluid in the legs. A person with failure of both ventricles has an enlarged heart that beats in gallop rhythm – that is, in groups of three sounds rather than two.

FACT FILE

Sometimes the heart valves become stiff or leaky. They can be replaced by valves made from tissue taken from an animal, or by artificial valves made of metal and plastic.

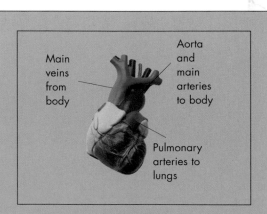

Main veins from body

Aorta and main arteries to body

Pulmonary arteries to lungs

WHEN DOES THE HEART STOP BEATING?

aorta

superior vena cava

pulmonary artery

pulmonary valve

pulmonary veins

atria

aortic valve

mitral valve

chordae tendineae

tricuspid valve

papillary muscle

ventricles

inferior vena cava

Your heart is a muscular pump that never stops beating. It has its own timing device that produces tiny electrical signals. These signals cause the heart muscle to contract rhythmically. The pump on the right side of the heart receives blood that has been pumped around the body. This blood is dark red and has used up most of its oxygen. The right pump sends it on a short circuit through the lungs that surround the heart. The blood comes back bright red and rich in oxygen, to the heart's left side, ready for its journey around the body. When the heart stops beating, body tissues no longer receive fresh blood carrying oxygen and nutrients. So life ends.

However, in a hospital, the cardiopulmonary machine can take over the job of heart and lungs. This means doctors can resuscitate people or carry out operations on the heart, such as replacing diseased valves.

FACT FILE

When the body is very active, the heart can pump 20 gallons of blood each minute. That would fill a bathtub within two minutes.

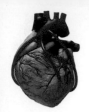

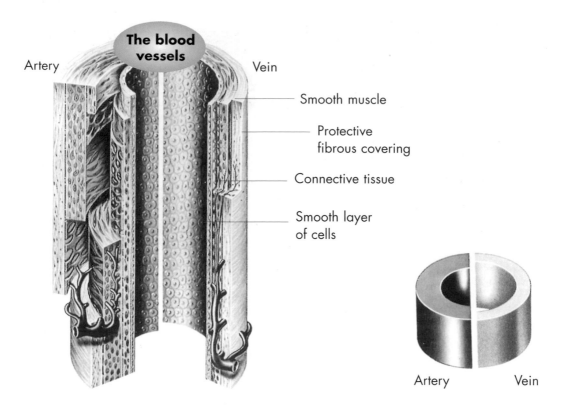

The blood vessels

Artery

Vein

Smooth muscle

Protective fibrous covering

Connective tissue

Smooth layer of cells

Artery   Vein

WHEN DOES BLOOD FLOW FROM VEINS TO ARTERIES?

Your body has an amazingly complex and delicate system of blood vessels, carrying blood to every nook and cranny, and then returning to the heart. These vessels are called arteries and veins and they are both tubes made up of four different layers. The arteries carry the blood away from the heart and the veins return it.

The veins frequently anastomose (or join together) with each other so that the blood flow can alter direction. This is caused if there is any constriction or pressure from movement of muscles or ligaments.

FACT FILE

Just over half of blood is plasma, which contains hundreds of dissolved substances, from sugars for energy, to hormones, to wastes like carbon dioxide.

WHEN DO RED AND WHITE BLOOD CELLS DIE?

FACT FILE

An adult body has about 5 litres of blood. At any time, about 1,250 ml are in the arteries, 3,500 ml in the veins and 250 ml in the capillaries. The blood cells flow through a capillary for only half a second before they move into the small veins.

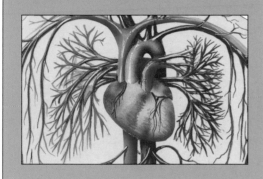

Both white and red blood cells are formed in the bone marrow. Each red blood cell measure about 7.5 microns (thousandths of a milli-metre) in diameter and are shaped a little like doughnuts. They contain haemoglobin, which gives their red pigment. There are 5 to 6 million red cells per cubic mm of blood. The red cell only survives about 120 days and the damaged and old cells are removed by the spleen and liver.

A white blood cell is not really white but almost transparent. It can change shape, push out folds and finger-like projections and move along by oozing and crawling like an amoeba in a pond. These cells survive less than a week.

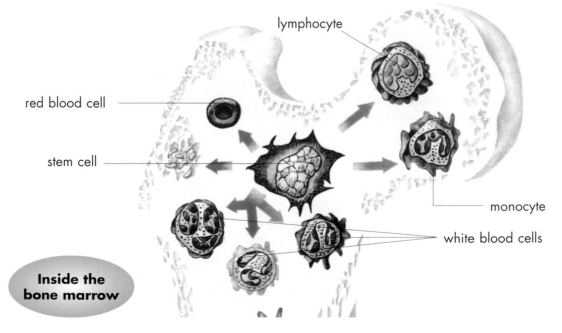

lymphocyte

red blood cell

stem cell

monocyte

white blood cells

Inside the bone marrow

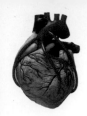

WHEN ARE OUR BLOOD GROUPS DETERMINED?

Receptor	A	B	AB	O
Donor A				
B				
AB				
O				

Our individual blood group is determined by our parents at the time of our conception. Blood groups are determined by the presence of antigens (a substance capable of stimulating an immune response) on the surfaces of the red cells. Although the red blood cells in different people look the same they are, in fact, dissimilar. They can be divided up into four main groups: A, B, AB and O.

Blood can be transplanted from one person to another by what we call a blood transfusion. It is very important that the blood given matches the person's group, because if the wrong types of blood are mixed together the result can be serious blood clots.

FACT FILE

Blood begins to clot as soon as it is exposed to the air, plugging the wound. White blood cells gather around the wound to kill invading microbes, and new skin cells grow into the healing wound beneath the scab.

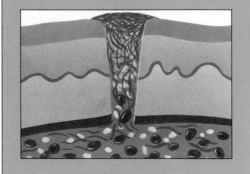

Brain & Nervous System

WHAT IS THE AUTONOMIC NERVOUS SYSTEM? 148
HOW DO NERVE IMPULSES WORK? 149

HOW ARE MESSAGES PASSED THROUGH THE NERVOUS SYSTEM? 150
HOW DOES THE BRAIN WORK? 151

HOW DOES MY MEMORY WORK? 152
WHERE IS THE CEREBRUM? 153

WHAT ARE THE AREAS OF THE BRAIN CALLED? 154
WHAT ARE THE THREE MAIN FUNCTIONS OF THE BRAIN? 155

WHAT CONTROLS OUR BALANCE? 156
WHAT CONTROLS OUR TEMPERATURE? 157

WHEN DOES OUR SENSE OF TOUCH ALERT THE BRAIN TO DANGER? 158
WHEN DO WE USE OUR BRAIN TO SMELL? 159

WHY DO WE DREAM? 160
WHY DO WE AWAKEN FROM SLEEP? 161

WHY DO WE GET THIRSTY? 162
WHY DO WE GET HUNGRY? 163

WHY ARE SOME PEOPLE LEFT-HANDED? 164

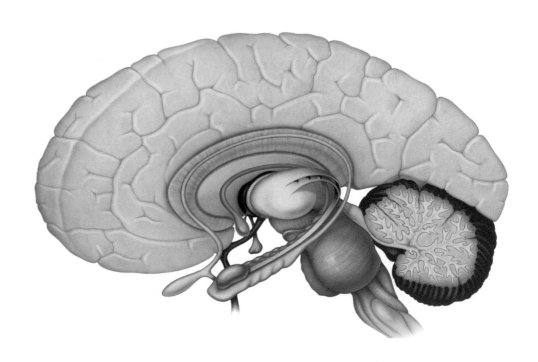

WHAT IS THE AUTONOMIC NERVOUS SYSTEM?

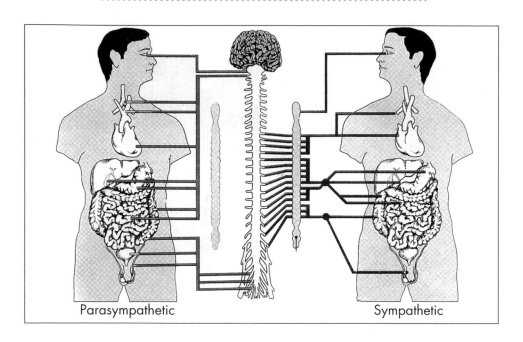

Parasympathetic

Sympathetic

There are many processes, like breathing and digestion, which it would be impossible for the body to regulate by conscious control from the brain. In order that these can function 'automatically', we have what is called an autonomic nervous system, which consists of two elements, the *sympathetic* and the *parasympathetic* system. The parasympathetic nerves tend to make the body calm and relaxed, and slow down processes such as digestion and heartbeat. The sympathetic nerves speed up all these processes and activities, so that the body is ready to spring into action. Between them, these two nerve sets fine-tune the body's internal conditions.

FACT FILE

The whole of the autonomic system is controlled by an area of the brain called the hypothalamus. This receives information about any variations in your body.

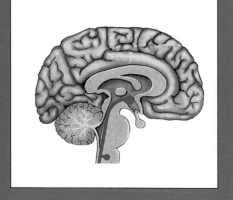

How do nerve impulses work?

A nerve impulse is like a very simple message: either on or off. Because there are so many neurones which are connected to one another, this simple signal is enough to carry the most complicated messages throughout the whole of the body's nervous system. As a nerve impulse arrives at the junction between two nerve cells, it is carried across the gap or synapse by chemicals called neurotransmitters. These contact sensitive areas in the next nerve cell, and the nerve impulse is carried along.

nerve gap (or synapse)

nerve membrane

neurotransmitter

arriving nerve impulse

Anatomy of a nerve cell junction

vesicle (stores drops of neurotransmitter)

FACT FILE

Scientists have produced maps showing how electrical activity in one part of the brain can cause a movement or other reaction. This mapping has been done during brain surgery. As there are no sense organs in the brain it is possible to operate on people who are fully conscious, without them feeling any pain. This enables doctors to know which part of the brain has been damaged after an accident.

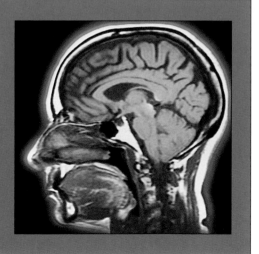

HOW ARE MESSAGES PASSED THROUGH THE NERVOUS SYSTEM?

Nerve impulses that pass through the nervous system are able to jump from one neurone to the next. Inside the nerve fibre, the nerve impulse travels as an electrical signal. When it reaches the end of the long fibre, it jumps across to the next neurone by means of a chemical transmitter. This chemical is released from the branched ends of the fibre. As this transmitter substance contacts the next neurone, it starts another nerve impulse. This whole process is very fast, and nerve impulses travel along the largest nerve fibres at 90m per second.

FACT FILE

A long thread or axon extends from the body of a neurone, and it is along this that nerve impulses are carried.

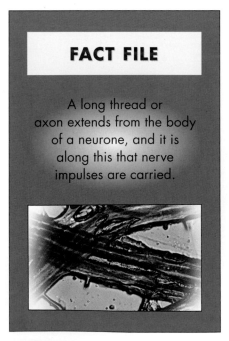

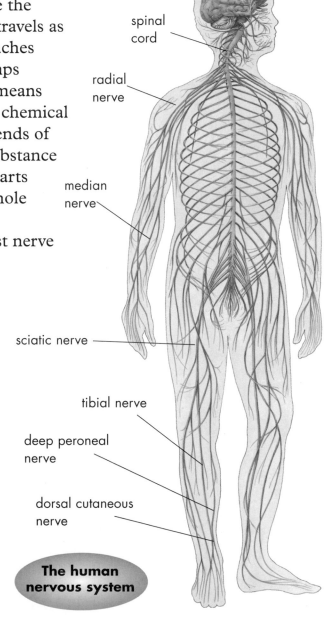

brain

spinal cord

radial nerve

median nerve

sciatic nerve

tibial nerve

deep peroneal nerve

dorsal cutaneous nerve

The human nervous system

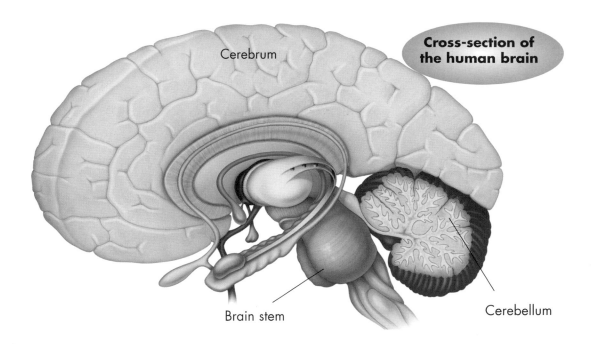

Cerebrum

Cross-section of the human brain

Brain stem

Cerebellum

HOW DOES THE BRAIN WORK?

FACT FILE

Each side of the brain controls the opposite side of the body. Usually the left side controls speaking, writing and logical thought, while the right controls artistic abilities. This musician is using the right side of his brain.

The brain is the body's control centre. It coordinates all the messages that pass through the nervous system, giving us the ability to learn, reason and feel. It also controls the body's automatic functions such as breathing, heartbeat, digestion, growth and blood pressure.

The brain is divided into three main regions each with a different function. The large part at the top is the cerebrum, where most of our thinking, reasoning and memory is controlled. The cerebellum is a smaller area at the back where both accurate movement and coordination are controlled. The brain stem is a small region at the base where most of our automatic body functions are processed and controlled.

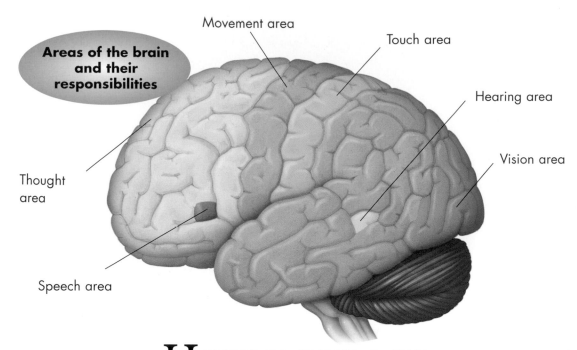

Areas of the brain and their responsibilities

Movement area

Touch area

Hearing area

Vision area

Thought area

Speech area

HOW DOES MY MEMORY WORK?

Memory is the ability to store things that you experience and learn, ready for use in the future. Some things are remembered easily, such as dramatic events in our life. However, more ordinary things need to be rehearsed several times before they 'stick'.

There are three different ways of storing memory. Sensory memory, which is very brief, tells you what is happening around you and allows you to move without bumping into things. Short-term memory, which lasts for only about 30 seconds, and allows you to remember a phone number and dial it, but after a minute or so it will vanish. Finally long-term memory, for things that you have carefully memorized and learned.

FACT FILE

The sense of smell has powerful effects in retrieving memories. Often a smell, like the burning of a bonfire, can suddenly trigger a memory from many years ago.

WHERE IS THE CEREBRUM?

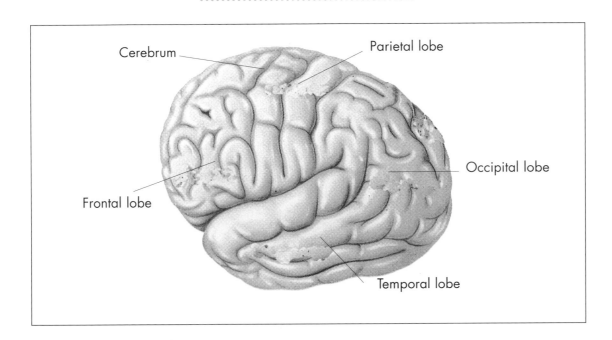

Cerebrum

Parietal lobe

Occipital lobe

Frontal lobe

Temporal lobe

FACT FILE

The brain stem is the vital control area of the brain and is concerned with maintaining all the essential regulatory mechanisms of the body: respiration, blood pressure, pulse rate, alertness and sleep.

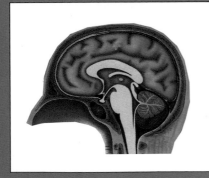

The cerebrum is part of the brain, representing about 85 percent of its weight. It's divided into two halves, the left cerebral hemisphere and the right cerebral hemisphere, by a conspicuous groove called the longitudinal fissure.

The hemispheres themselves are joined by bundles of nerves, the largest being the corpus callosum, and are in turn divided into four lobes. The frontal lobe is at the front, the temporal lobe at the lower side, the parietal lobe in the middle and the occipital lobe at the back, each of these names being the same as the bone of the skull that it lies beneath.

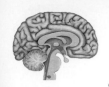

WHAT ARE THE AREAS OF THE BRAIN CALLED?

Basically the brain can be divided into three different regions: hindbrain, midbrain and forebrain. Each of these regions is in turn divided into separate areas responsible for quite distinct functions, all intricately linked to other parts of the brain.

The largest structure in the hindbrain is called the cerebellum. The largest part of the entire brain is the cerebrum, which is located in the forebrain. It is more developed in humans than in any other animal. This is where the other parts of the brain send incoming messages for decision. The cerebral cortex is the thick wrinkled layer of grey matter folded over the outside of the cerebrum. This part of the brain has become so highly developed in humans that it has had to fold over and over in order to fit inside the skull. Unfolded, it would cover an area 30 times as large as when folded.

FACT FILE

Shivering is governed by four mechanisms. The hypothalamus, at the base of the brain, senses that the temperature is too low and sends messages to the thyroid gland, telling it to speed up the metabolic rate. The body muscles then alternately contract and relax rapidly, thus producing heat. The nerves then send messages to the skin and the skin pores narrow, ensuring that the heat is conserved within the body.

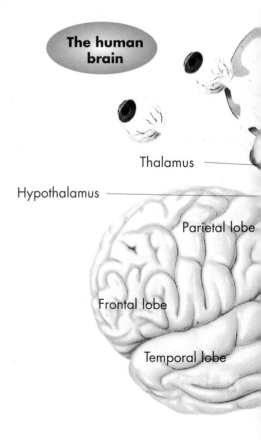

The human brain

Thalamus

Hypothalamus

Parietal lobe

Frontal lobe

Temporal lobe

WHAT ARE THE THREE MAIN FUNCTIONS OF THE BRAIN?

The brain is the body's control centre. It keeps the body working smoothly and it looks after thoughts, feelings and memory.

Different parts of the brain have different jobs to do. The largest part is called the cerebrum, or forebrain. It looks like a huge half-walnut. The cerebrum's main job is to sort out and respond to messages sent to it from the senses. It also stores information, as memory, and it thinks. Messages from the senses are managed by the cerebrum's sensory area, while the motor area controls the muscles.

Thinking, memory and speech are managed by the parts known as the association areas. The cerebellum (or hindbrain) is below the cerebrum. It works with the cerebrum's motor area to ensure that the muscles function smoothly.

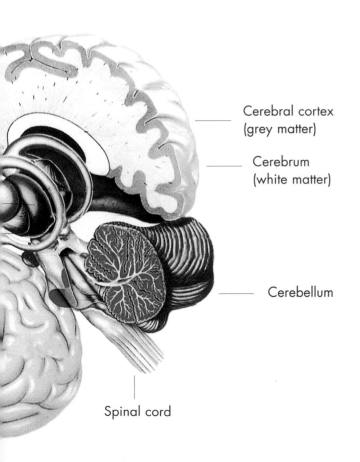

Cerebral cortex
(grey matter)

Cerebrum
(white matter)

Cerebellum

Spinal cord

FACT FILE

Although we have invented computers that can work out millions of different things in seconds, our brains can still outwork and outsmart them! Our brains control our bodies by sending out billions of tiny electrical signals every second.

WHAT CONTROLS OUR BALANCE?

The inner ear is the body's main organ of balance, but the brain also receives messages from nerve-endings in the neck, back, leg and feet muscles. The brain sifts all this information and sends messages back to the muscles, allowing us to perform incredible feats of balance such as ice-skating or gymnastics. Near the cochlea are fluid-filled tubes – the semicircular canals. As your head moves about, the fluid inside each canal swishes to and fro. When the body moves, the fluid causes hairs in a jelly-like mass to bend. These are connected to the vestibular nerve, which alerts the brain to re-balance the body.

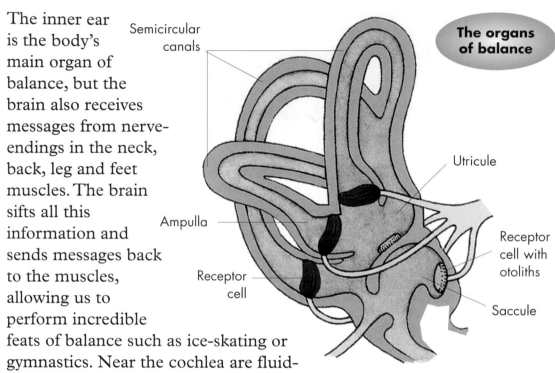

Semicircular canals

The organs of balance

Utricule

Ampulla

Receptor cell with otoliths

Receptor cell

Saccule

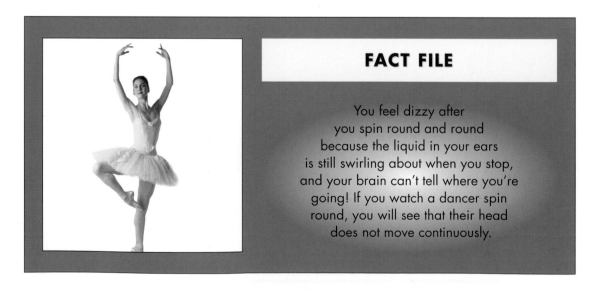

FACT FILE

You feel dizzy after you spin round and round because the liquid in your ears is still swirling about when you stop, and your brain can't tell where you're going! If you watch a dancer spin round, you will see that their head does not move continuously.

WHAT CONTROLS OUR TEMPERATURE?

FACT FILE

Body movements can also be homeostatic. A hot person may spread out arms and legs to increase heat loss; a cold person curls up to reduce the areas of the body losing warmth.

The name for 'constancy of the internal environment' is homeostasis. The body must regulate many body systems and processes to keep inner conditions stable. The temperature nucleus in the hypothalamus controls heat loss and production by the body through the skin. Overheating (A) causes an increased blood flow from the blood vessels (1), to radiate heat and causes sweating through the sweat glands (2), to lose heat. A fall in body temperature (B) constricts the surface blood vessels, stops sweating and makes the erector muscles (3) contract, causing the hairs (4) to stand on end, trapping air as an insulating layer. Additional heat can be produced by shivering.

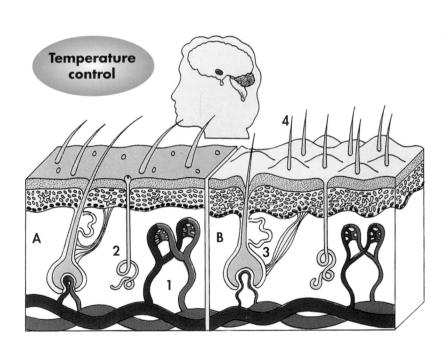

Temperature control

WHEN DOES OUR SENSE OF TOUCH ALERT THE BRAIN TO DANGER?

Close your eyes and touch something, such as your clothes, a table, a car or even your own skin. Stroke it gently. What does it feel like? Is it hard or soft, hot or cold? The surface may be smooth, bumpy, gritty, furry or hairy. It could be dry, moist, or slimy. Your skin continuously passes huge amounts of information to the brain. It monitors touch, pain, temperature and other factors that tell the brain exactly how the body is being affected by its environment. Without this constant flow of information, you would keep injuring yourself accidentally, which is what happens in some rare diseases where the skin senses are lost. Senses in the skin are measured by tiny receptors at the ends of nerves. There are several different types of receptor. Each type can detect only one kind of sensation, such as pain, temperature, pressure, touch and so on.

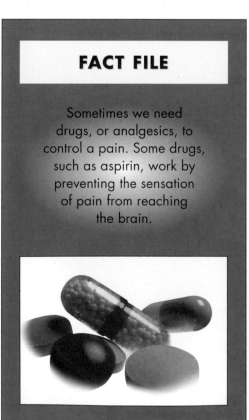

FACT FILE

Sometimes we need drugs, or analgesics, to control a pain. Some drugs, such as aspirin, work by preventing the sensation of pain from reaching the brain.

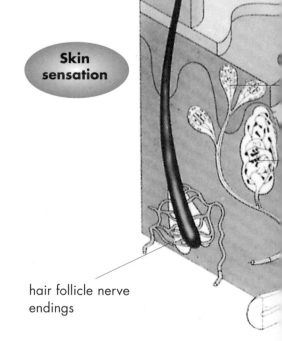

Skin sensation

hair follicle nerve endings

WHEN DO WE USE OUR BRAIN TO SMELL?

The part of the brain that analyzes messages coming from the receiver cells in the nose is closely connected with the limbic system, that part of the brain that deals with emotions, moods and memory. It is called the primitive brain, sometimes even the 'smelling brain'. The connection explains why smells are richly supplied with emotional significance. The smell of fresh rain on a summer's day usually makes people feel happy and invigorated, and it may also evoke happy memories. The smell of fresh-baked bread may bring on instant pangs of hunger, while the scent of perfume may remind you of a loved one. On the other hand, unpleasant smells such as rotten eggs, produce revulsion and sometimes even nausea.

Certain smells will bring memories of long forgotten special occasions flooding back, as we tend to remember those things which have special emotional significance. This is because the areas of the brain which process memories are also closely linked to the limbic system, which in turn is linked to the areas in the brain that control the sense of smell.

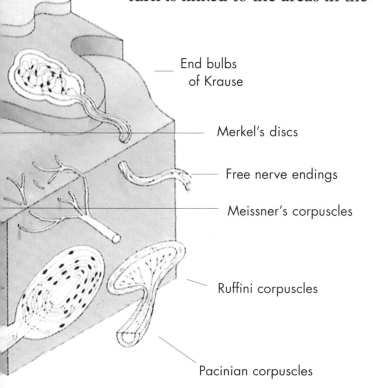

End bulbs of Krause

Merkel's discs

Free nerve endings

Meissner's corpuscles

Ruffini corpuscles

Pacinian corpuscles

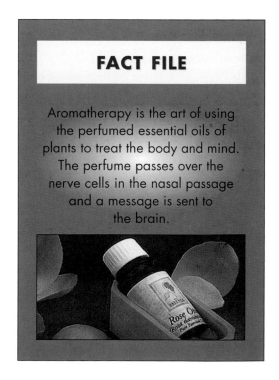

FACT FILE

Aromatherapy is the art of using the perfumed essential oils of plants to treat the body and mind. The perfume passes over the nerve cells in the nasal passage and a message is sent to the brain.

WHY DO WE DREAM?

Whatever we dream, it is touched by our feelings, wishes, memories, fears and emotions. But other influences can come into play as well; if something is impacting physically, like cold or hunger, it can often be a part of our dreams. We've all heard of someone (if not ourselves) who has fallen out of bed and dreamt they were falling off a cliff just as they woke up. Psychoanalysts study the reasons for us dreaming, saying that dreams reflect wishes that didn't come true, that a dream is a form of wish fulfillment. According to this line of thought, when we are asleep our inhibitions are also asleep.

FACT FILE

Daydreaming is actually a form of dreaming, only it is done while we are awake. Night dreaming is done while we are asleep. That is the only difference between them, since both are done when the dreamer is so relaxed that he pays no attention to what goes on around him.

WHY DO WE AWAKEN FROM SLEEP?

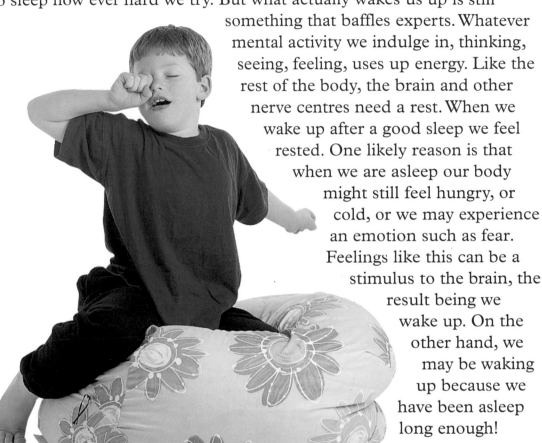

There are some things about sleep that even scientists find hard to explain. Sometimes we 'drop off' in an instant, other times we can't get to sleep how ever hard we try. But what actually wakes us up is still something that baffles experts. Whatever mental activity we indulge in, thinking, seeing, feeling, uses up energy. Like the rest of the body, the brain and other nerve centres need a rest. When we wake up after a good sleep we feel rested. One likely reason is that when we are asleep our body might still feel hungry, or cold, or we may experience an emotion such as fear. Feelings like this can be a stimulus to the brain, the result being we wake up. On the other hand, we may be waking up because we have been asleep long enough!

FACT FILE

Even while the body sleeps, its nerve systems are active, continuously monitoring and adjusting the internal processes, and checking the outside world for danger. The heart never stops, but beats slower while at rest.

WHY DO WE GET THIRSTY?

All of us have had the experience of being thirsty at times, but can you imagine how it would feel to be thirsty for days? If a human being has absolutely nothing to drink for a long period, he or she will die. Thirst is simply our body's way of telling us to replenish its liquid supply.

The reason for this thirst is caused by a change in the salt content of our blood. There is a certain normal amount of salt and water in our blood. When this changes by having more salt in relation to water in our blood, thirst results.

There is a part of our brain called the 'thirst centre'. It responds to the amount of salt in our blood. When there is a change, it sends messages to the back of the throat. From there, messages go to the brain, and it is this combination of feelings that makes us say we are thirsty.

FACT FILE

Onions send out an irritating substance when we peel them. The onion has an oil containing sulphur which not only gives it its sharp odour, but it also irritates the eye. The eye reacts by blinking and producing tears to wash it away. That is why we cry when we peel onions.

WHY DO WE GET HUNGRY?

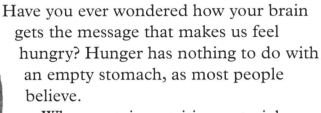

Have you ever wondered how your brain gets the message that makes us feel hungry? Hunger has nothing to do with an empty stomach, as most people believe.

When certain nutritive materials are missing from the blood, hunger sets in. The lack of these materials in the blood vessels results in a message being sent to a part of the brain called the 'hunger centre'. The hunger centre is a bit like a brake that works on the stomach and the intestine, if there is enough food for the blood the hunger centre slows up the action of the stomach and intestine. When food is missing from the blood, it stimulates the stomach and intestine into more anction. That is why when we are hungry we often hear our stomach rumbling.

When we are hungry, we don't want any particular kind of food, our body just needs nourishment. It depends on the individual how long we can actually live without food. A very calm person can live longer than an excitable one because the protein stored up in his body is used up more slowly.

FACT FILE

Eggs are an extremely good form of protein, which is vital for the building up and repair of muscles. Milk and dairy products are another good source of protein.

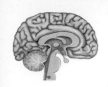

WHY ARE SOME PEOPLE LEFT-HANDED?

About four per cent of the population is left-handed. In the course of history many of the greatest geniuses have also been left-handed. Leonardo da Vinci and Michelangelo, two of the greatest artists of all time, were both left-handed.

The brain has a right half and a left half and these two do not function in the same way. It is believed that the left half of the brain is predominant over the right half.

As the left half of the brain predominates, the right half of the body is more skilled and better able to do things. We read, write, speak, and work with the left half of our brain. And this, of course, makes most of us right-handed too. But in the case of left-handed people, it works the other way around. The right half of the brain is predominant, and such a person works best with the left side of his body.

FACT FILE

Did you know that no two human beings have the same set of fingerprints? A fingerprint is the pattern formed by the ridges on the layers of skin at the tips of your fingers. If you press your finger on an ink pad and then onto a piece of paper, you should be able to see some of these patterns.

Genetics & Reproduction

WHAT HAPPENS TO A FERTILIZED EGG? 166
WHAT ARE CHROMOSOMES? 167

HOW DOES SKIN COLOUR DIFFER? 168
HOW DO WE GET BROWN EYES? 169

WHEN IS A BABY'S GENETIC MAKE-UP DECIDED? 170
WHEN DOES MITOSIS OCCUR? 171

WHEN WERE GENES DISCOVERED? 172
WHEN DO WE LEARN TO TALK? 173

WHERE DOES A BABY DEVELOP? 174
WHEN ARE TWINS CONCEIVED? 175

WHERE IS SPERM PRODUCED? 176
WHERE DOES MENSTRUATION TAKE PLACE? 177

WHY DO WE HAVE CHROMOSOMES? 178
WHERE DO WE INHERIT OUR TRAITS? 179

WHAT HAPPENS TO A FERTILIZED EGG?

A fertilized egg (or zygote) goes through a series of changes before it reaches the uterus. In the uterus, the zygote develops into a form called the embryo, which develops rapidly. The zygote then travels through the fallopian tube toward the uterus. Along the way, the zygote begins to divide rapidly into many cells with no increase in overall size. The resulting cell mass is called a *morula*. By the third or fourth day the morula enters the uterus and the embryo

Morula

develops from the central cells of the morula. They develop into the placenta, a special organ that enables the embryo to obtain food and oxygen from the mother. After the morula enters the uterus, it continues to divide. At this stage, the ball of cells is called a *blastocyst*. The cells of the blastocyst divide as it floats in the uterus for one or two days. About the fifth or sixth day of pregnancy, the blastocyst becomes attached to the internal surface of the uterus. The

Blastocyst

outer cells of the blastocyst, called the *trophoblast*, secrete an enzyme that breaks down the lining of the uterus. The trophoblast begins to divide rapidly, invading the uterine tissue. The process of attachment to the uterine wall is called implantation.

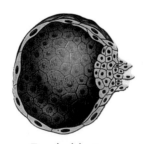

Trophoblast

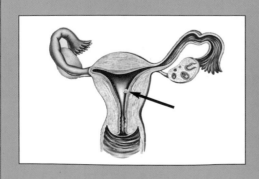

FACT FILE

By the 11th day of the pregnancy, the blastocyst is firmly implanted in the uterus. Various structures develop in the uterus to help the embryo grow. These structures include the placenta and certain membranes.

WHAT ARE CHROMOSOMES?

The moment of conception is the most important stage of sexual reproduction. Fertilization is complete when the chromosomes of the

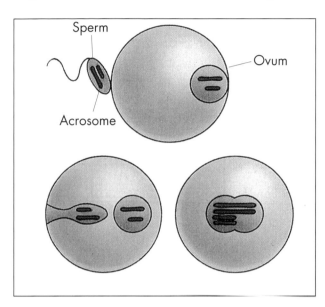

Sperm

Ovum

Acrosome

male sperm unite with the chromosomes of the female egg. Chromosomes are threadlike structures that contain genes, the units of heredity that determine each person's unique traits. Most body cells have 46 chromosomes that occur in 23 pairs. However, as each egg or sperm develops, it undergoes a special series of cell divisions called meiosis. As a result, each sperm or egg cell

contains only one member of each chromosome pair, or 23 unpaired chromosomes. During fertilization, the chromosomes pair up so that the fertilized egg has the normal number of 46 chromosomes. Only about 100 sperm survive the journey of nearly 24 hours and only one fertilizes the ovum. The sperm's acrosome disappears as it dissolves the membrane of the ovum. The tail and body are shed when the head penetrates to join its 23 chromosomes with those of the ovarian nucleus.

FACT FILE

Special sex chromosomes determine whether the zygote will develop into a boy or a girl. Each body cell contains a pair of sex chromosomes. In females, the two sex chromosomes are identical.

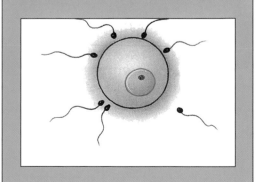

HOW DOES OUR BODY GROW?

The most important forces that cause growth lie inside a living thing from the beginning. These forces are called its heredity. The human body has stages of growth: embryo and foetus, infant, child, youth, mature adult and old age. People's bodies grow faster in the early weeks of life than at any other time. Even before the end of the first year, they are growing less rapidly. Through the whole period of childhood, they grow at a moderate rate. Then growth starts to speed up again. All human beings are much alike in their growth. But there are important differences. Boys and girls all follow the same general pathway of growth, but each individual follows it in their own way.

Growth stages of a human foetus before birth

4 weeks

8 weeks

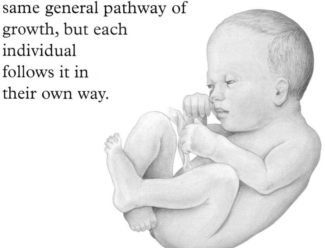

12 weeks

20 weeks

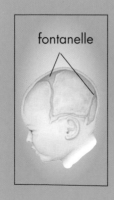

fontanelle

FACT FILE

The bones of a baby's head are not fused at birth, making the skull flexible enough to pass through the mother's birth canal. The bones eventually join, but a gap in the skull, called the fontanelle, may not close up for several months.

30 weeks

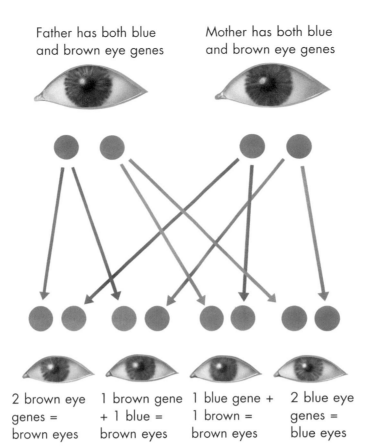

Father has both blue and brown eye genes

Mother has both blue and brown eye genes

2 brown eye genes = brown eyes

1 brown gene + 1 blue = brown eyes

1 blue gene + 1 brown = brown eyes

2 blue eye genes = blue eyes

HOW DO WE GET BROWN EYES?

FACT FILE

This DNA molecule is shaped like a ladder twisted into a spiral. The pattern in which these are formed is the code built into the DNA molecule and groups of these form genes.

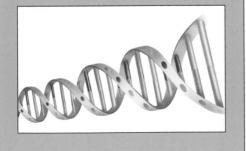

Although genes from both parents are mixed together at fertilization, some genes have a more powerful effect than others. These dominant genes override the effects of others which are called recessive genes. For example, if a child has a gene for brown eyes from one parent, and a gene for blue eyes from the other, the child will always have brown eyes. This is because the gene for brown eyes is a dominant gene.

However, two parents with brown eyes may have children with blue eyes if the parents carry the blue eyes. This means that a child would get the recessive blue gene from both parents.

WHEN IS A BABY'S GENETIC MAKE-UP DECIDED?

A baby's genetic make-up is decided right from the time when the egg is fertilized. A very important part of cell division involves the nucleus. Each nucleus contains two sets of genes. One came originally from the person's father and one from the mother. So before a cell divides, both sets of genes are copied. This is termed DNA replication. Each new offspring cell then receives a full double set of genes, one from the father and one from the mother.

Because each human body gets half its genes from each parent it inherits some of the features of each parent. This is why all kinds of characteristics, for example height, run in families.

However, every human body has its own unique physical circumstances, such as the food we eat, our environment and the illnesses that we catch.

We also each have our own behavioural and mental development. So we inherit a mix of physical features from our parents, but also we are all individual and unique.

FACT FILE

A long thread or axon extends from the body of a neurone, and it is along this that the nerve impulses are carried.

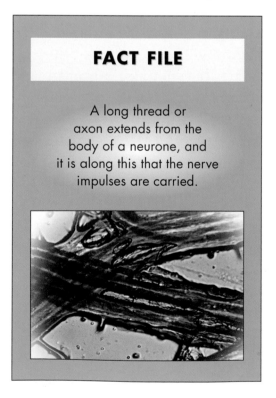

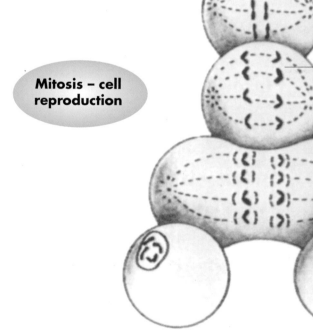

Mitosis – cell reproduction

WHEN DOES MITOSIS OCCUR?

As well as being packed with information, the DNA of chromosomes also has the ability to reproduce itself. Without this, the cells could not pass on information from one generation to the other. The process of cell division in which the cell duplicates itself is called mitosis, which works as follows:

1. the chromosomes become shorter and the nuclear envelope breaks,
2. the chromosomes are released, which duplicate and attach themselves to a cytoplasmic network,
3. they are then drawn apart
4–7 to form two new cells with reformed nuclear envelopes.

Mitosis is absolutely essential to life because it provides new cells for growth and for replacement of worn out cells. Mitosis may take minutes or hours, depending upon the kind of cells and species of organisms. It is influenced by time of day, temperature, and chemicals. Strictly speaking the term mitosis is used to describe the duplication and distribution of chromosomes, the structures that carry our genetic information.

(1) (2) (3) (4) (5) (6) (7)

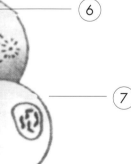

FACT FILE

DNA strands look like a twisted ladder. Sections of DNA are called genes. All the instructions for growing a new human being are coded into the DNA molecule.

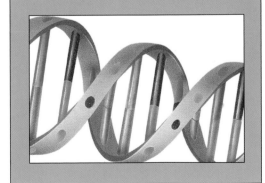

WHEN WERE GENES DISCOVERED?

In the 1800s a monk named Gregor Mendel experimented with characteristics in pea plants by cross-fertilizing plants with different traits. He kept a careful track of the traits displayed by the pea plants produced by cross-fertilization, discovering that the characteristics from the parent plants were inherited by the progeny plants in specific patterns.

Mendel also discovered during his experiments that certain genes seemed more dominant than others. For example if a pea with a white flower is cross-fertilized with a pea with a pink flower, the resulting flowers will all be pink.

This is obvious in human beings. For example, if a child has a gene for brown eyes from one parent and a gene for blue eyes from the other, the child will always have brown eyes. This is because the gene for brown eyes is a dominant gene.

Model of DNA

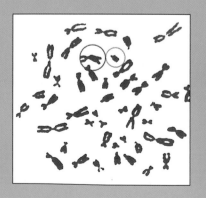

FACT FILE

Chromosomes are tiny threads that are present in all cells apart from red blood cells. They contain all the information for an entire person to develop. There are 46 chromosomes in each cell. They come in 22 pairs, plus another special pair that determine the person's sex.

WHEN DO WE LEARN TO TALK?

As air flows out of the lungs, we can use it to make the sounds of speech and other noises. At the top of the windpipe, in the sides of the voice box or larynx, are two stiff, shelf-like folds – called the vocal cords. Criss-crossed muscles in the voice box can pull them together so that air passes through a narrow slit between them and makes them vibrate, creating sounds. As the vocal cords are pulled tighter, they make higher-pitched sounds. As the vocal cords loosen, they make lower-pitched sounds. Of course, when we actually learn to talk, our speech depends on the development of the brain and its ability to copy the sounds that we hear.

FACT FILE

Although many people think of speech as our main way of communicating, we do not have to use spoken words. People who can't speak learn a language called signing, in which hands and fingers are used to signal letters and words.

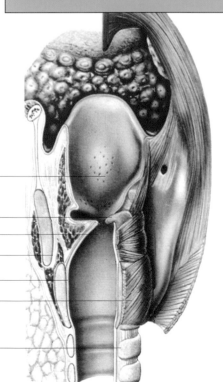

epiglottis

vocal cord

larynx

thyroid cartilage

thyroid cartilage

cricoid cartilage

Organs of speech

trachea: C-shaped cartilages

WHERE DOES A BABY DEVELOP?

A baby develops in the uterus, or womb – a hollow, muscular organ in the mother's abdomen. The period of development in the uterus lasts about nine months in most cases. During this period, development is more rapid than at any time after birth.

For a baby to develop, a sperm from the father must unite with an egg from the mother. This union of a sperm and an egg is called fertilization. It produces a single cell called a fertilized egg. By a series of remarkable changes, the fertilized egg gradually develops into a baby.

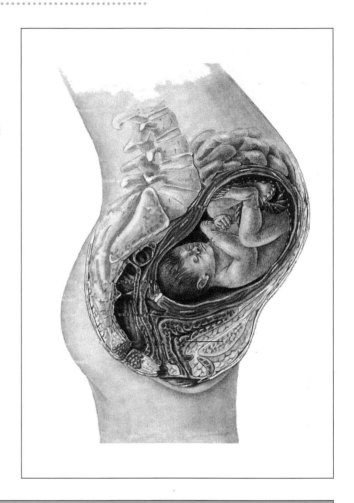

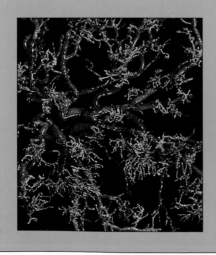

FACT FILE

The placenta is an organ composed largely of blood vessels. The placenta is attached to the wall of the uterus. A tube-like structure called the umbilical cord joins the placenta to the embryo at the abdomen. The placenta supplies everything that the embryo needs to live and grow.

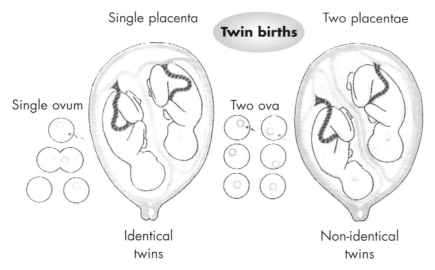

Single placenta   **Twin births**   Two placentae

Single ovum   Two ova

Identical twins   Non-identical twins

WHEN ARE TWINS CONCEIVED?

A baby begins as a fertilized egg – a pinhead-sized egg cell from the mother, which has joined an even smaller tadpole-shaped sperm cell from the father. Although thousands of these sperm cells may cluster around the egg cell, only one of these will actually fertilize the egg.

Non-identical twins are produced when two eggs are released at the same time, and both are fertilized. They can be the same sex, or brother and sister.

Identical twins are produced when the embryo splits into two in the early stages of its development. This produces two identical children of the same sex. Some identical twins look so alike that they can only be told apart by their fingerprints.

Only one in 83 pregnancies results in twins.

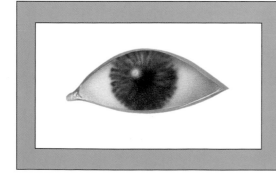

FACT FILE

Identical twins share the same physical traits: identical eye colour, hair colour and other characteristics. Non-identical twins are only as alike as any other pair of siblings.

WHERE IS SPERM PRODUCED?

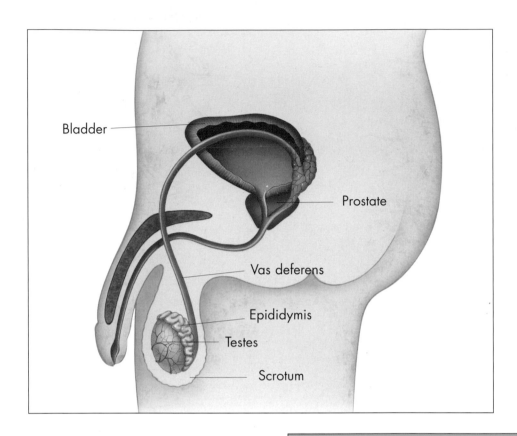

Bladder

Prostate

Vas deferens

Epididymis

Testes

Scrotum

Sperm, the male sex cells, develop in the testes. It is stored for several days until needed. The testes contain long tubes called the seminiferous tubules, which are tightly coiled. Sperm is produced continuously in these tubes, then passed to the epididymis and stored in a large duct called the vas deferens. Here liquid is added to the sperm to make a milky fluid called semen. It is stored in pouches called seminal vesicles. During sexual intercourse the seminal vesicles contract and force out the sperm.

FACT FILE

Up to 100 million sperms are produced every day by the male. If they are not released they are soon destroyed and replaced. Sperms look like tiny tadpoles with rounded heads and long lashing tails.

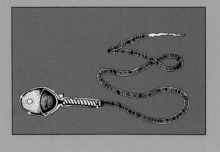

WHERE DOES MENSTRUATION TAKE PLACE?

FACT FILE

The ovary is one of a pair of female sex organs that store and release eggs. The human ovary is oval in shape and about the size of an unshelled walnut.

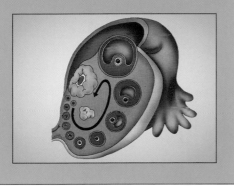

Most women of child-bearing age experience menstruation, the loss of blood and cells through the vagina that takes place on a monthly basis. The uterus, or womb, is the oval-shaped organ that holds a baby during pregnancy, and each month blood and cells build up in its lining. This lining thickens in preparation for pregnancy, and when pregnancy does not happen, the lining breaks down. The blood and cells are then discharged through a canal that leads from the uterus to the outside of the body; this canal is the vagina. The menstruation process can last over a period of anything from three to seven days, this time being known as the menstrual period.

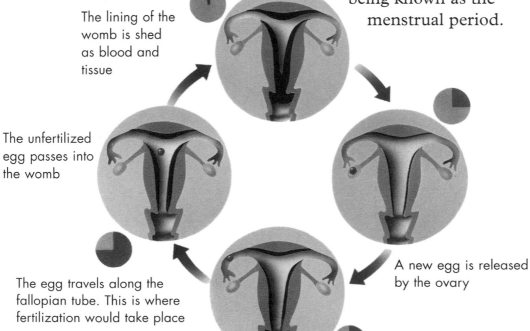

The lining of the womb is shed as blood and tissue

The unfertilized egg passes into the womb

The egg travels along the fallopian tube. This is where fertilization would take place

A new egg is released by the ovary

WHY DO WE HAVE CHROMOSOMES?

Every cell has a nucleus which is full of information coded in the form of a chemical called deoxyribonucleic acid (or DNA). The DNA is organized into groups called genes. Every chromosome contains thousands of genes, each with enough information for the production of one protein. This protein may have a small effect within the cell and on the appearance of the body. It may make all the difference between a person having brown or blue eyes, or straight or curly hair.

At the moment the mother's egg is fertilized, the genes start issuing instructions for the moulding of a new human being. Every characteristic which we inherit from our parents is passed on to us through the coding of the genes within the chromosomes.

In rare cases, some people have 47 chromosomes. This occurs when people inherit Downs Syndrome, a genetic disorder.

FACT FILE

A baby starts when two special cells meet – a sperm cell from a man's body and an egg cell from a woman's body. Joined inside the woman's body, these two cells grow into a whole new person.

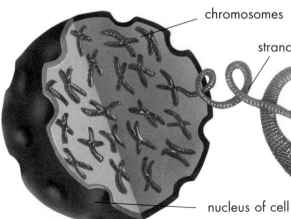

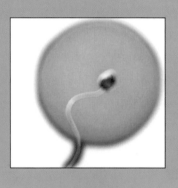

chromosomes

strand of chromosome

nucleus of cell

rings of pairs of amino acids

DNA strand looks like a twisted ladder

WHERE DO WE INHERIT OUR TRAITS?

Living things inherit characteristics, often called traits, from their parents through heredity. Heredity is the passing on of biological characteristics from one generation to the next. The process of heredity occurs among all living things – animals, plants and even such microscopic organisms as bacteria. Heredity explains why a human mother always has a human baby and why a mother dog has puppies and not kittens. It is also the reason offspring look like their parents. You resemble your parents because you inherited your hair, nose shape and other traits from them. All organisms consist of cells. Tiny biochemical structures inside each cell called genes carry traits from one generation to the next.

FACT FILE

You may look like your parents, but you are not an exact duplicate of either of them. You inherited half your genes from your father and half from your mother.

History

Who?

WHO WERE THE FRANKS? 182
WHO WERE THE HITTITES? 183

WHO DID THE ANCIENT GREEKS WORSHIP? 184
WHO WAS ALFRED THE GREAT? 185

WHO WAS THE FIRST NORMAN KING OF ENGLAND? 186
WHO WERE THE CELTS? 187

WHO FORMED THE 'NEW MODEL ARMY'? 188
WHO INTRODUCED PERESTROIKA AND GLASNOST? 189

WHO GAVE THE GETTYSBURG ADDRESS? 190
WHO FOUNDED FASCISM? 191

WHO WERE THE SUMERIANS? 192
WHO WAS ALEXANDER THE GREAT? 193

WHO WAS BOADICEA? 194

WHO WERE THE FRANKS?

Frankish soldiers

The Franks emerged from the ruins of the Roman Empire in AD 476 as the dominant people of western Europe. Their leader, Clovis, enlarged his lands around the River Rhine in Germany through war. By AD 540 the Franks ruled most of the old Roman province of Gaul (France, named after the Franks).

The first Frankish ruling family is known as the Merovingian dynasty, after Clovis's grandfather Meroveus. Clovis became a Christian. He made Paris his capital city. Most of the Franks were peasant farmers, who lived on lands ruled by nobles. The peasants raised food, doing the seasonal tasks of ploughing, sowing and harvesting. They also had to fight for their lord when he went to war. The Frankish system of land-holding and service was the beginning of the feudal system in Europe.

Charlemagne was king of the Franks from 768 to 814, and created a vast empire. On Christmas Day in 800 the pope crowned Charlemagne Holy Roman Emperor. After the rule of Charlemagne the Frankish empire began to break up.

FACT FILE

The Frankish king Charlemagne introduced this writing, called 'Carolingian script', which was easier for people to read and write.

WHO WERE THE HITTITES?

Hittite charioteers

The Hittites arrived in what is now Anatolia in Turkey, from either central Europe or central Asia in about 2000 BC, and during the next 500 years, expanded their territory to parts of Syria in the south and Mesopotamia in the east. Like the Sumerians and Egyptians, they could muster huge armies, and were among the first people to use chariots in war, from which archers fired arrows, giving them an edge over enemies.

One of the first battles for which accounts remain, happened in 1282 BC at Kadesh on the Orontes River. Mutwatallis, the Hittite leader, fought a battle against Egyptian forces under Rameses II. The Hittites were winning, but Rameses managed to regroup when the Hittites stopped fighting to loot Egyptian equipment. Both sides claimed it as a victory, it was inconclusive and the two sides signed a non-aggression treaty.

FACT FILE

The Hittites were the first to master iron-making, and this can be seen in their weaponry. Axe heads were made from bronze (shown here) and also iron.

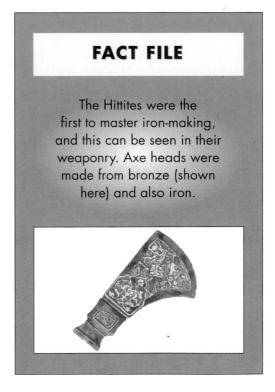

WHO DID THE ANCIENT GREEKS WORSHIP?

The Greeks believed in many different gods, chief among these were a family of supernatural beings who lived on Mount Olympus and watched over humanity. Certain gods looked after the harvest; others cared for wild animals, the sea, war and such like. King of the gods was Zeus, whom the Romans called Jupiter. The first Olympic Games, which took place in 776 BC, were held in his acclaim. Greeks believed that the universe was a sphere. The upper half was light and airy, the lower half dark and gloomy, and the Earth was a flat disc, floating between the two halves. When people died they went to the Underworld, which was ruled by Hades, the brother of Zeus. Poseidon was the Greek god of the sea, and is often shown carrying a three-pronged spear, called a trident. The Greeks believed Poseidon to be the brother of Zeus and Hades. He was also associated with earthquakes and horses, and the Greeks thought that he was the father of the winged horse, Pegasus.

Zeus

Poseidon

FACT FILE

The ruins of Greek and Roman temples can be seen across Europe, the Near East and North Africa. Every town had its own temple, dedicated to a protector god or goddess.

WHO WAS ALFRED THE GREAT?

FACT FILE

The Alfred jewel was found near Athelney in Somerset in 1693. It may be part of a bookmark. On it are the words 'Alfred had me made' in Latin.

In the late ninth century, most of the northeastern half of England was under the control of the Danish Vikings. The West Saxons had been at war with them for years when Alfred the Great (849 to 899) came to the throne in 871. After years of war, Alfred reconquered London in 886, made peace with the Vikings and began the process of uniting the kingdoms of England under his leadership.

With more resources at his disposal, Alfred could fortify strategic points and protect the coast with a large fleet.

Alfred was an effective peacetime ruler: parts of his code of laws are still recognizable in the English legal system. He also encouraged learning and literature, as well as the translation of Christian texts into Old English to promote a cultural revival in England.

WHO WAS THE FIRST NORMAN KING OF ENGLAND?

The first Norman king of England was William I, the Conqueror (1027 to 1087). He was born in about 1027 in Falaise in Normandy, the son of Duke Robert I, and became duke on his father's death in 1035.

In 1066, after the death of Edward the Confessor, William claimed the English throne had been granted to him by Edward and when the latter's brother-in-law, Harold was elected to the throne by the English nobles, William had no choice but to invade. William's army won the battle known as the Battle of Hastings on October 14. William was crowned in Westminster Abbey on Christmas Day. From the start, he ruled with an iron fist, taking lands from the Saxons. In 1086, he commissioned the great survey of every property in the country – the Domesday Survey. He started what became known as the feudal system: in return for grants of land, his followers had to swear allegiance and supply men for military service. Their followers had to do likewise, right down the social scale to the serfs (slaves).

FACT FILE

At the Battle of Hastings the English, who fought on foot, resisted as Norman cavalry charged their shield wall and fired arrows at them. When the Normans feigned retreat, the English chased them downhill and were slaughtered. This is recorded in 72 scenes on the Bayeux Tapestry.

WHO WERE THE CELTS?

The Celts came from central Europe, although their previous origins are unclear. Around 500 BC, perhaps to escape wars with their Germanic neighbours, they began to move westwards. Groups of people settled in what are now Spain, France, Britain and Ireland. Celts were warlike and their arrival usually led to fighting.

The Celts were artistic people. They loved stories and music, and they made beautiful jewellery and metalwork decorated with abstract designs and animal shapes.

They had no written language, passing on their legends of gods and heroes in stories around the fire. Most of what we know of the Celts today comes from the writings of their enemies, such as the Romans. The Celts themselves left a legacy of art and legend, and language: Welsh, Breton, Cornish, Irish and Scottish Gaelic are all Celtic languages.

An example of Celtic art

FACT FILE

The Celts often constructed their settlements on hilltops, which could be easily defended. They are identified by circular defensive ditches that still survive in former Celtic areas.

WHO FORMED THE 'NEW MODEL ARMY'?

Oliver Cromwell (1599 to 1658), led the armed forces of Parliament to victory in the English Civil War against the royalists in the 1640s.

Cromwell was a military genius. In the winter of 1644 and 1645, when the war was at a stalemate, he purged the Parliamentarian high command of those he felt were not helping their cause. Cromwell's friends persuaded Parliament to establish a full-time professional force, the New Model Army, under Sir Thomas Fairfax, with Cromwell as general. The New Model Army (or the Roundheads) was a disciplined fighting force and never lost a major battle. At the Battle of Naseby, in Northamptonshire (June 14, 1645), it destroyed the king's main field army. Cromwell earned the nickname 'Ironsides'.

FACT FILE

The term Roundhead originally referred to the parliamentary infantryman, with his hair cut short to fit his casque (steel helmet). By the end of the English Civil War, the armies of Parliament were superior in cavalry and infantry.

WHO INTRODUCED PERESTROIKA AND GLASNOST?

What are *perestroika* and *glasnost*? They formed part of the policies of Mikhail Gorbachev, the last leader of the Soviet Union. After his appointment in 1985, Gorbachev proposed reforms of the Soviet political and economic system. Everything was controlled from the centre by the Communist Party and he wished to increase the power of elected bodies and modernize the economy. This programme was called *perestroika* (restructuring). *Glasnost* means 'openness', which he wanted the Soviet Union to have internally and with other nations.

In 1990, Gorbachev received the Nobel Peace Prize for his reforms and arms limitations agreements with the United States of America, but the Soviet Union broke up in 1991.

FACT FILE

The US President Ronald Reagan was a keen supporter of Gorbachev's programme of reforms in the USSR. In 1987 the two leaders signed an agreement to dismantle many kinds of nuclear weapon.

WHO GAVE THE GETTYSBURG ADDRESS?

Abraham Lincoln (1809 to 1865) was the sixteenth president of the United States and one of the great leaders in American history. A humane, far-sighted statesman in his lifetime, he became a legend and a folk hero after his death.

Lincoln delivered the short speech that has become known as the Gettysburg address on November 19, 1863, at the site of the Civil War Battle of Gettysburg in Pennsylvania. The occasion was a dedication ceremony for a cemetery for the Union soldiers who died there in the three-day bloodbath four months earlier.

The aim of the speech was to rouse the spirits of the Union and to affirm the reasons why the Northern States were fighting the war against the Confederate states.

FACT FILE

Abraham Lincoln was against slavery, and his election convinced the leaders of the southern states that the only option to them was to leave the Union. South Carolina was the first state to leave in 1860, soon followed by Mississippi, Florida, Alabama, Georgia and Louisiana.

WHO FOUNDED FASCISM?

Fascism was a political movement founded in Italy by Benito Mussolini (1883 to 1945) in 1919. His brand of revolutionary nationalism – nationalization and putting Italy's interests first – were popular with old soldiers. In 1921, he transformed the *Fasci di Combattimento* into the National Fascist Party, and in 1922 his black-shirts marched on Rome and secured his appointment as prime minister. He imposed one-party rule with himself as dictator.

He delayed involving Italy in World War II until 1940, when a German victory seemed probable. Five years later, after Italy's defeat, he was executed by Italian partisans.

FACT FILE

Sir Oswald Mosley formed the British Union of Fascists in 1932. His views were violently anti-Semitic and his black-shirted followers rioted in areas with strong Jewish communities, such as London's East End. He was interned in World War II because of his support for Hitler.

WHO WERE THE SUMERIANS?

About 7,000 years ago, farmers began to move into an area of land between the Tigris and the Euphrates rivers. This fertile land was called Mesopotamia, in what is now called Iraq. In the south of Mesopotamia was the land known as Sumer. The Sumerians, as they became known, were a very inventive race. They developed the first form of writing and recording numbers.

The Sumerians drew pictures on soft clay with a pointed reed. The pictures were drawn downwards in lines, from the right-hand side. Later, they started to write across the tablet from left to right. The reed tip became wedge shaped, as did the marks it made.

FACT FILE

Reed houses were built using reeds cut down from the marshes around the Tigris and Euphrates rivers. The Sumerians also made canoes from these reeds.

WHO WAS ALEXANDER THE GREAT?

Alexander the Great (356 to 323 BC) was king of the Macedonians and was one of the greatest generals in history. He came to the throne in 336 BC, and after consolidating his power in Greece, two years later began his conquest of the Persian Empire. By 328 BC he had reached India, but in 327 BC had to turn back because his soldiers were threatening to mutiny after almost ten years away from home. Alexander's conquests furthered the cross-fertilization of Greek and Persian ideas and customs in western Asia and Egypt. His empire did not last beyond his death in Babylon in 323 BC. It was split up into a number of smaller kingdoms ruled by his friends and allies.

FACT FILE

Alexander imposed a single system of money throughout his lands. He was keen to promote trade and commerce across the empire too.

WHO WAS BOADICEA?

Boadicea (Boudicca) was the queen of the Iceni, a tribe of Celts living in eastern England. Her husband was a governor, who worked with the Romans. After his death the Romans tried to take control. Boadicea led a rebellion, which sacked the towns of Colchester and London, until the Roman armies marched against her. The Romans defeated the Iceni and their Celtic allies. Boadicea is renowned for fighting from a chariot, and the Romans had to develop special tactics to combat these fast-moving warriors. Boadicea ended her own life by taking poison to avoid being captured.

FACT FILE

Celtic poetry:

'STORM AT SEA'
Tempest on the plain of Lir
Bursts its barriers far and near
And upon the rising tide
Wind and noisy winter ride
Winter throws a shining spear.

Queen Boadicea on her chariot

How?

. . . .

HOW WAS ROME FOUNDED? 196
HOW VAST WAS THE ROMAN EMPIRE? 197

HOW SUCCESSFUL WERE VIKING ATTACKS? 198
HOW FAR DID THE VIKINGS TRAVEL? 199

HOW DID THE NORMANS CHANGE BRITAIN? 200
HOW DOES THE DOMESDAY BOOK HELP HISTORIANS? 201

HOW DID THE MONGOLS LIVE? 202
HOW EXTENSIVE WAS THE MONGOL EMPIRE? 203

HOW LONG WAS THE HUNDRED YEARS WAR? 204
HOW WIDESPREAD WAS THE BLACK DEATH? 205

HOW DID THE INDUSTRIAL REVOLUTION CHANGE BRITAIN? 206
HOW SIGNIFICANT WAS THE INVENTION OF THE STEAM ENGINE? 207

HOW DID WORLD WAR I BEGIN? 208
HOW DID NEW TECHNOLOGY INFLUENCE WORLD WAR I? 209

HOW DID WORLD WAR II BEGIN? 210
HOW STRONG WAS NAZI FIGHTING POWER? 211

HOW DID THE UNITED NATIONS BEGIN? 212

HOW WAS ROME FOUNDED?

According to the legend, Rome was founded in 753 BC by twin brothers called Romulus and Remus. The babies were raised by a she-wolf, having been abandoned by their uncle on the banks of the River Tiber. They were eventually rescued by a shepherd.

By 509 BC the original Etruscan inhabitants of Rome had been driven out, and by 275 BC Rome controlled most of Italy. The Phoenicians were great rivals of Rome, and they were finally defeated by the Romans in the Punic Wars (261 to 146 BC). After this, the Romans were able to extend their empire with little organized resistance. The Celts, the Seleucid kings, the Greeks and the Egyptians all fell before Roman power. Only the Parthians in the east and the Germanic tribes in northwest Europe defied the mighty Roman army.

FACT FILE

Part of the complex of Roman baths in the city of Bath in England. Romans would visit the public baths to bathe in hot and cold pools, and also to relax and talk with their friends.

HOW VAST WAS THE ROMAN EMPIRE?

At its peak, the Roman army extended all around the Mediterranean Sea and most of the rest of Europe. Much of what is now England and France, Belgium and the Netherlands, Spain and Portugal, Switzerland, Austria, Hungary, part of Germany, Romania, Bulgaria, Greece, Turkey, Israel, Syria, Arabia, Tunisia, Algeria, and Morocco was ruled by the Romans from their base in Italy.

A huge army was needed to maintain control over these regions, and the costs were tremendous. There were continual minor wars and skirmishes along the edges of the Empire, which meant that large garrisons of soldiers had to be maintained.

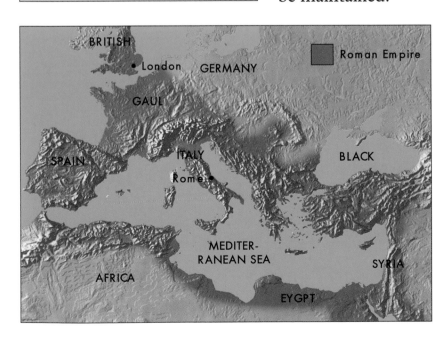

HOW SUCCESSFUL WERE VIKING ATTACKS?

The Vikings came from Scandinavia (Norway, Denmark and Sweden). Their homeland of mountains, fjords and forests offered little spare farmland for a growing population, so many Vikings went abroad in search of new lands to settle.

They were fierce warriors and their first impact on western Europe was a violent one. Norwegians and Danes began to sail across the North Sea in the late AD 700s, raiding the coasts of Britain and mainland Europe. They raided churches and towns, carrying off loot and slaves. Their raids caused panic and rulers tried to buy off the invaders with gold, known as Danegeld. This only encouraged the Vikings to come back for more.

In Britain, the Vikings were finally defeated by Alfred, the king of Wessex.

FACT FILE

Religion was important to the Vikings. Their most important gods were Odin, Thor and Grey. Odin, the god of battle, was the leader of the Norse gods, who lived in a place called Valhalla.

HOW FAR DID THE VIKINGS TRAVEL?

FACT FILE

The Viking longships were fast and strong enough to cross oceans. They had a long, slender hull with a single mast and sail.

At a time when sailors dared not venture far from the coasts, the Vikings boldly sailed out far across the Atlantic in their small open longships. Viking trade routes took them throughout Europe and beyond. The Vikings travelled as far east as Baghdad and Istanbul, and as far west as Greenland and Canada. Wherever Vikings landed they mingled with local people, and they began to set up colonies in Iceland and Greenland and sailed on to North America. Traces of Viking settlements have also been found in Maine, in the United States, and in Newfoundland in Canada. However, these colonies soon vanished, together with the colony in Greenland. Other Vikings sailed around the Mediterranean, trading for goods from places as far away as China.

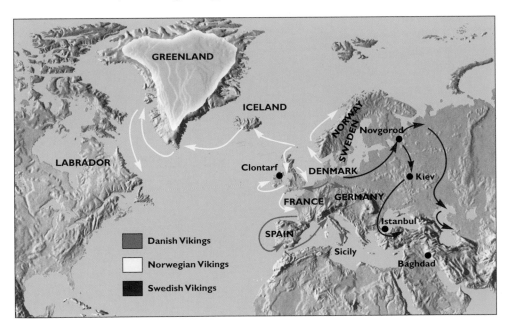

GREENLAND

ICELAND

NORWAY

SWEDEN

Novgorod

LABRADOR

Clontarf

DENMARK

Kiev

FRANCE   GERMANY

Istanbul

SPAIN

Sicily

Baghdad

Danish Vikings

Norwegian Vikings

Swedish Vikings

HOW DID THE NORMANS CHANGE BRITAIN?

The Bayeux tapestry records the Norman victory over the Saxon King Harold, who is shown here receiving the fatal arrow in his eye.

FACT FILE

Knights were soldiers in the service of a Norman lord. They owed their loyalty to their lord and had to fight for him whenever asked. This meant that the knights were called upon in times of unrest.

The Normans introduced the feudal system to England. According to this system, the king owned all the land and others could hold land in exchange for providing services to the king. William the Conqueror appointed barons who were provided with estates taken from the original English earls. In return, the barons paid him taxes and supplied soldiers for his armies.

The barons, in turn, let their knights hold smaller sections of land, while the knights let part of this land to people called villeins. They were farmers who had to provide some of their produce to the local lord of the manor. In this way, the land and the whole of English society was broken into small, easily controlled units.

HOW DOES THE DOMESDAY BOOK HELP HISTORIANS?

The Domesday Book

Once the Normans had secured their hold over their new territory, they wanted to know exactly what it was worth. In AD 1085 William I ordered a survey of land in England. The findings were written down in the Domesday Book (Domesday means 'Day of Judgement'). It is the best record we have of life in England between AD 1066 and 1088, naming about 13,000 towns and villages.

This book listed every single town, village, farm, who owned what, and how much each hold was worth, so that taxes could be applied. This book is still in existence today.

FACT FILE

Conwy castle, in north Wales, is typical of the castles built by the Normans. It was built to give defending archers an uninterrupted field of fire against any attackers, and could withstand a long siege.

HOW DID THE MONGOLS LIVE?

The Mongols never settled permanently, but lived in large circular tent-like prefabricated homes called yurts.

These were carried with them during their migrations and invasions, and are still used today. They are made of felt, which is fastened over a light wooden frame. The whole structure can be quickly dismantled and carried by horses as the Mongol tribes migrate across the steppes, or grassy plains, following their grazing flocks.

The Mongols were feared for the ferocity of their unpredictable attacks on cities throughout Asia and the Middle East. Genghis Khan was a famous Mongol who unified the scattered tribes and began the conquest that resulted in the Mongols controlling nearly all of Asia and threatening to destroy Europe. After the death of Genghis' grandson, Kublai, the Empire proved too large to govern and began to break up.

FACT FILE

This is an example of a Mongol home called a yurt, which they carried with them during their migrations and invasions.

HOW EXTENSIVE WAS THE MONGOL EMPIRE?

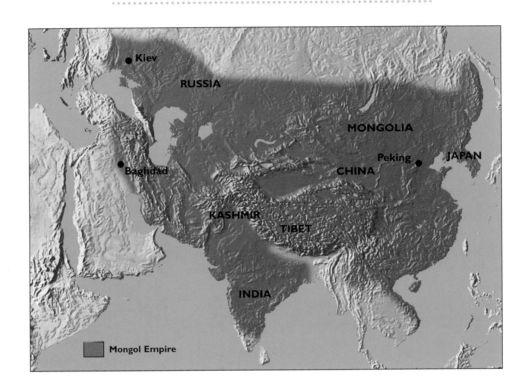

Kiev

RUSSIA

MONGOLIA

Baghdad

Peking JAPAN

CHINA

KASHMIR

TIBET

INDIA

Mongol Empire

The vast Mongol empire stretched across central Asia from the sea of Japan to the Caspian Sea and occupying most of modern Russia. The Mongols succeeded against established armies because they were unpredictable. They charged into battle on horseback, relying entirely on speed and surprise, and taking no prisoners. The Mongols were remorseless fighters, developing fighting machines that enabled them to break into the cities they besieged. They were merciless towards those people who resisted them and sometimes they slaughtered entire populations. Most cities surrendered immediately, rather than risk being massacred!

FACT FILE

Marco Polo was one of the first Europeans to travel through Mongol territory. His reports helped to establish trade routes there.

HOW DID AMERICA BECOME INDEPENDENT?

Resentment against taxes imposed on the American colonies by Britain finally led to the Declaration of Independence, and in the following war, the Americans finally gained full independence of British rule.

The new American nation consisted of 13 states (this has now grown to 50). It had a president, who would be elected every four years, and was run by a Congress. This same structure exists to the present day.

FACT FILE

Eleven Confederate states (orange) broke away from the Union (green) fearing the abolition of slavery. Five slave states (red) stayed in the Union, although some of their people supported the Confederacy.

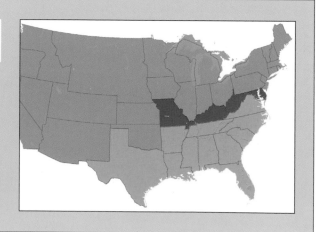

HOW DID THE AMERICAN INDIANS LOSE THEIR LAND?

FACT FILE

The American flag was originally designed with thirteen stars and thirteen stripes to represent the original colonies that signed the Declaration of Independence. With each new state, another star is added to the flag.

The Native American Indians understandably resented the numbers of settlers who swarmed onto their traditional hunting and grazing lands. As the population of the United States grew rapidly, the Indians were forced to migrate to the south and west. Soon they had nowhere left to go and began to fight back.

The US government reacted by forcing the American Indians into reservations on land that was not wanted by the settlers. Many Indians died fighting trying to save their land, or from starvation and disease.

The huge herds of buffalo on which many Indians depended were hunted by the settlers, depriving them of their main source of food, clothing and shelter.

HOW DID THE INDUSTRIAL REVOLUTION CHANGE BRITAIN?

Back in the early eighteenth century, Britain was still largely an agricultural nation. The few manufactured goods were made in small workshops or at home. As a result of Britain's world trading, the cotton industry developed and everything changed. At first, water power was used to drive spinning and weaving machines, and factories and mills were set up. New towns were built to provide homes for the workers. Steam engines were adapted to provide power to factories. The railway and canal system were developed. The other key development was the smelting of iron using coke rather than wood. Britain was able to exploit the raw materials from her overseas empire to become one the world's most prosperous industrial nations.

FACT FILE

Trade with the Far East involved a long voyage around the tip of Africa. The Suez Canal provided a quick route through the Mediterranean and the Red Sea.

HOW SIGNIFICANT WAS THE INVENTION OF THE STEAM ENGINE?

The invention of practical steam engines was the most significant advance in the eighteenth century, providing power for the Industrial Revolution. The first steam engines were massive stationary devices that pumped water from flooded mines, but they were soon adapted to power vessels.

The first steam locomotives appeared in the early nineteenth century. They carried goods and allowed people to travel to factories where they worked. Trains were an important means for social change because, for the first time, people could travel quickly and visit areas that were previously too far away.

FACT FILE

Steam locomotion also made overseas trading possible. One of the most important exports was tea, which was in great demand in Europe.

HOW DID WORLD WAR I BEGIN?

Continual trouble in the Balkans led to the formation of several complicated military alliances throughout Europe. The continent was eventually split into two groups. Britain, France and later Russia joined to form the Entente Cordiale, while Germany, Austria-Hungary and Italy formed the Triple Alliance. In 1914 Archduke Franz Ferdinand of Austria-Hungary was assassinated in Serbia, activating the alliance agreements. First Austria declared war on Serbia, Russia sided with Serbia, and then Germany declared war on Russia. Germany invaded Belgium, bringing the British and French into the conflict.

FACT FILE

The Versailles Treaty ended World War I, but its terms were so severe that Germany suffered economic collapse and this caused resentment that was to build up and eventually contribute to the causes of World War II.

Central Powers

Allies

Neutral nations

NORWAY

SWEDEN

IRELAND

DENMARK

RUSSIA

BRITISH ISLES

NETHERLANDS

GERMANY

BELGIUM

Paris

AUSTRO-HUNGARIAN EMPIRE

SWITZERLAND

FRANCE

ROMANIA

PORTUGAL

SERBIA

BULGARIA

SPAIN

ITALY

ALBANIA

OTTOMAN EMPIRE

Mediterranean Sea

GREECE

HOW DID NEW TECHNOLOGY INFLUENCE WORLD WAR I?

World War I was the first mechanized war in history. In the beginning, fighting was similar to wars fought in the previous century. But new and terrifying weapons were introduced, which completely changed the whole style of warfare.

Aircraft were used for the first time to observe the enemy and to locate suitable targets for the long-range artillery. Later on, fighter planes began to shoot down the spotters, introducing aerial warfare. Aircraft and Zeppelin airships were used as bombers.

The most terrifying new weapon was poison gas, which was used by both sides. It caused millions of deaths and terrible suffering. Tanks also made their first appearance.

FACT FILE

The war brought the first armoured tanks into battle. They could break through enemy lines and create openings for troops. Earlier use of tanks could have saved lives and helped shorten the war.

HOW DID WORLD
WAR II BEGIN?

As in World War I, some international alliances were activated following the German invasion of Poland. As a result of this, Britain and France declared war on Germany.

When the Germans attacked Poland, the Russians also attacked the country and it was divided.

The Germans went on to invade Denmark, Norway, Belgium, The Netherlands and France in quick succession. They crushed any resistance with overwhelming armoured forces.

World War II killed more people than any other war in history. The fighting spread to nearly every part of the world and included nearly 60 nations.

The Americans entered the war in 1941 after being attacked by Germany's ally Japan. At this time a huge military build-up began in England.

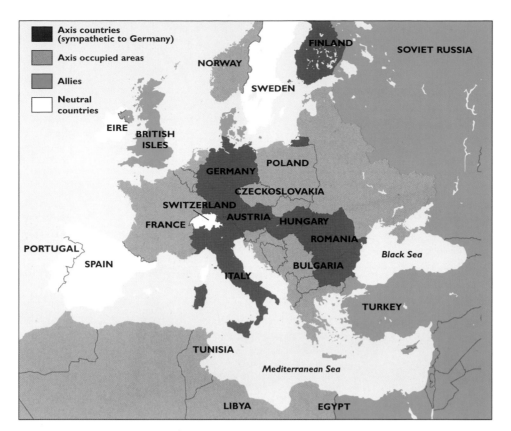

Axis countries (sympathetic to Germany)

Axis occupied areas

Allies

Neutral countries

NORWAY
FINLAND
SOVIET RUSSIA
SWEDEN
EIRE
BRITISH ISLES
POLAND
GERMANY
CZECHOSLOVAKIA
SWITZERLAND
AUSTRIA
HUNGARY
FRANCE
ROMANIA
PORTUGAL
SPAIN
BULGARIA
Black Sea
ITALY
TURKEY
TUNISIA
Mediterranean Sea
LIBYA
EGYPT

HOW STRONG WAS NAZI FIGHTING POWER?

FACT FILE

The greatest military operation ever carried out was the invasion of Europe by the Allied forces in 1944, when millions of troops were ferried across the Channel and landed from floating harbours on the shores of France.

When the Germans realized that the British defences were too strong for their aircraft, they tried to destroy British industry. They hoped to damage the morale of the British population by night bombing of the cities. The German Luftwaffe, which was considered to be far superior to the RAF, set out to bomb the British airfields and shoot down their aircraft. The Luftwaffe abandoned its attempts to defeat the RAF when they realized they were flying too far from home and ran short of fuel. As part of their policy to 'purify' the German race, the Nazis had a plan to exterminate the Jews.

HOW DID THE UNITED NATIONS BEGIN?

The flag of the
United Nations

During World War II, the Allied nations referred to themselves as the 'United Nations'. In 1942 they agreed that they would not make any separate peace agreements with Germany.

It was the Potsdam Conference in 1945 that really laid the ground for the foundation of the United Nations to prevent future conflict and also set out procedures for the prosecution of Nazi war criminals. Twenty-seven countries signed this first agreement and in 1945, after the war, the United Nations formally came into existence with an initial membership of fifty countries.

The United Nations (UN) is led by a powerful Security Council, which can intervene in international disputes that might lead to conflict. Today the UN is also involved in many economic aid programmes around the world.

FACT FILE

Early in 1945 the Allied leaders met in Yalta in the Crimea to decide on the post-war shape of the world. Churchill, Roosevelt and Stalin decided on how Germany was to be split up once the war was won.

What?

WHAT DID EARLY EXPLORERS USE FOR NAVIGATION? 214
WHAT WAS DAILY LIFE LIKE IN ANCIENT GREECE? 215

WHAT WAS THE MAGNA CARTA? 216
WHAT WAS THE BLACK DEATH? 217

WHAT WAS STEPHENSON'S ROCKET? 218
WHAT WAS THE WOMEN'S MOVEMENT? 219

WHAT WERE NINETEENTH-CENTURY SLUMS LIKE? 220
WHAT WAS THE GREAT DEPRESSION? 221

WHAT WAS THE TREATY OF VERSAILLES? 222
WHAT WAS THE EASTER RISING? 223

WHAT WAS THE BATTLE OF BRITAIN? 224
WHAT WAS THE HOLOCAUST? 225

WHAT WAS THE BLITZKRIEG? 226
WHAT IS COMMUNISM? 227

WHAT WAS THE CUBAN MISSILE CRISIS? 228

WHAT DID EARLY EXPLORERS USE FOR NAVIGATION?

An astrolabe

Early astronomers and navigators used astrolabes to measure the angles of celestial bodies above the horizon. A metal disk mounted on a circular frame is suspended vertically and the observer looks through the sights to line up a star and then measures its position against the marks on the frame. He can then use tables to work out his postion. The astrolabe remained in use from the time of the ancient Greeks until the seventeenth century, when it was replaced by more accurate instruments such as the sextant.

People probably made rough maps even before they began to use written language some 5,500 years ago. Over the centuries, maps became more accurate as people explored the world and developed improved ways to make maps. An early map of the world appeared in a 1482 edition of Ptolemy's eight-volume *Geography*.

FACT FILE

Ferdinand Magellan was a Portuguese sea captain who commanded the first expedition that sailed around the world. His voyage provided the first positive proof that the Earth is round. Many scholars consider it the greatest navigational feat in history.

WHAT WAS DAILY LIFE LIKE IN ANCIENT GREECE?

Much of what we know about how the Greeks lived comes from pictures on vases. The pictures not only show wars and stories from mythology, but also daily activities such as hunting, farming and fishing. Greek homes were built around a central courtyard, cool and airy, where the family slaves prepared food on an open fire. There was a small shrine to the household god. Many houses were made without windows in the outer walls. This design kept out both the hot sun and thieves. People ate with their fingers, while lying on wooden couches. Slaves brought in the dishes of food, while a musician played on pipes or a lyre. Men and women wore a *chiton*, a cloth square draped over the body and fastened by a pin at the shoulder.

FACT FILE

A portrait of a Greek woman on a fragment of pottery. Greek women spent most of their time around the home organizing the household.

WHAT WAS THE MAGNA CARTA?

The youngest son of Henry II, John, inherited from his brother Richard the throne of England, as well as the Plantagenet dominions of France, which he had lost to the French by 1204. John's failure to recapture these territories, his dispute with Rome over the Pope's choice of a new Archbishop of Canterbury, and a high level of taxation, had the English nobility up in arms against him.

Magna Carta

In 1215 they forced the King to agree to the Magna Carta, guaranteeing their rights in relation to those of the crown. It was intended to protect the rights of nobles, and made sure that no-one was imprisoned without a fair trial. Copies of this document, which tried to put an end to the king's abuse of his power, were distributed across the whole of England. This led to civil war, which only ended with John's death in 1216.

Despite all these disasters, it is now known that John was a much better king than history has actually portrayed him.

John

FACT FILE

The magnificent coronation of Charles V. He became king of Spain in 1516 (he was the grandson of King Ferdinand and Queen Isabella of Spain), and three years later he was crowned Holy Roman Emperor.

Infected houses were marked with an 'X'

WHAT WAS THE BLACK DEATH?

The bubonic plague (or 'Black Death') was a deadly disease, which brought death to most parts of Asia, North Africa and Europe. The first outbreak was recorded in 1331 in China. The plague started as a bloody swelling in the armpit or groin and quickly invaded the whole body. It was highly contagious and killed millions of people. The infection probably began on the steppes, the grassy plains of Asia. It was carried by fleas, which lived in the fur of the black rat. The rats lived close to humans and thus the disease spread rapidly. Corpses were left out in the road for people to collect, thus spreading the disease even further.

FACT FILE

Medieval paintings often depicted death as a skeleton, dancing and leading victims to their end. The epidemic killed at least 25,000,000 people in Europe and the Near East.

WHAT WAS STEPHENSON'S ROCKET?

FACT FILE

In 1840, the American inventor Samuel F. B. Morse launched a code based on dots, dashes and spaces. Known as the Morse code, it speeded up the sending of messages through the telegraph.

Modern rail travel owes its existence to the great engineer George Stephenson. While working as a mechanic in a coal mine, he educated himself at night school. By 1812, he was a chief mechanic and, in 1814, he built his first locomotive, the Blucher.

This locomotive propelled itself at 4 miles (6 km) per hour and could pull eight wagons loaded with coal. Stephenson refined the steam engine until, in 1829, he built the first practical steam locomotive, the Rocket. It could travel at an amazing 36 miles (58 km) per hour.

George Stephenson

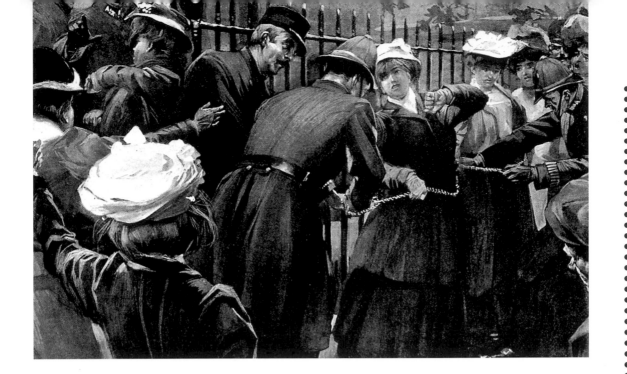

WHAT WAS THE WOMEN'S MOVEMENT?

FACT FILE

In Britain, the suffragette campaigners often went on hunger strike when imprisoned for their actions. The authorities did not want them to die, and arouse public sympathy, so they fed the women by force.

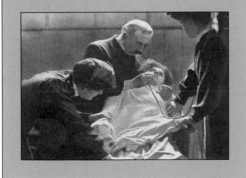

The women's movement had its roots in the late eighteenth and early nineteenth centuries. The American and French revolutions promoted ideas of 'equality' and 'liberty', yet women could not vote, and had limited access to education.

In 1792, a British writer called Mary Wollstonecraft published *A Vindication of the Rights of Women*, setting out her belief in equal rights for men and women. This idea took a firm hold during the 1800s, and many women started to campaign for reform. The suffragettes engaged in many different forms of protest, including chaining themselves to railings outside the residence of the British Prime Minister.

WHAT WERE NINETEENTH-CENTURY SLUMS LIKE?

The events of the Industrial Revolution brought great changes to towns and cities in Britain. People needed to live close to their workplace, so huge numbers of houses were put up to accommodate this new class of industrial worker. The speed with which many towns and cities expanded led to problems with overcrowding, and dirty and insanitary housing. Many workers were forced to live in slum conditions. Worse, the new factories created pollution that often contaminated both water supplies and the air. Early industrial cities were disease-ridden places with very high death rates.

FACT FILE

Life in the industrial centres revolved around the mines, mills and factories where people worked.

Pollution from the new factories

WHAT WAS THE GREAT DEPRESSION?

A disastrous stock market crash in 1929 in the USA left many people penniless overnight. The effects of the Wall Street Crash were felt all over the world. Many countries in Europe were hard hit because they had borrowed money from the USA at the end of World War I. Throughout the 1930s, unemployment soared and trade slumped in a period known as the Great Depression.

During the worst years of the Depression, many people were forced to rely on charity and government hand-outs for their most basic needs. In 1932 Franklin D. Roosevelt was elected US present. His 'New Deal' aimed to create jobs and to protect people's savings by regulating banks more closely.

FACT FILE

This is the Stock Exchange in Wall Street at the time of its collapse. You can see brokers spilling out onto the streets of the city of New York.

WHAT WAS THE TREATY OF VERSAILLES?

The signing of the Treaty of Versailles

FACT FILE

The signing of the Treaty of Versailles on June 28, 1919, in Paris, was the fifth anniversary of the shooting of Archduke Ferdinand in Sarajevo.

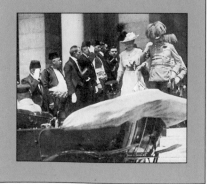

The Treaty of Versailles was a peace document signed at the end of World War I by the Allied and Associated Powers and by Germany. It took place in the Hall of Mirrors in the Palace of Versailles, France, on June 28, 1919 and actually came into force on January 10, 1920.

The treaty was drafted during the Paris Peace Conference in the spring of 1919, which was dominated by the national leaders known as the 'Big Four', David Lloyd George of Britain, Georges Clemenceau of France, Woodrow Wilson of the United States and Vittorio Orlando of Italy. They wanted to make sure that Germany would never again pose a military threat. The treaty contained a number of stipulations to guarantee this.

WHAT WAS THE EASTER RISING?

FACT FILE

The British Prime Minister, David Lloyd George, proposed that Ireland would stay under British control, but the Irish Free State would become a British dominion.

During World War I, the issue of Home Rule continued to cause conflict in Ireland. When war actually broke out in 1914, most Irish Volunteers supported Britain in its fight against the Central Powers. But a breakaway group formed the Irish Republican Brotherhood (later known as the IRA). On Easter Monday, 1916, protesters belonging to this and other nationalist movements seized buildings in Dublin and proclaimed Ireland a republic. This rebellion became known as the Easter Rising.

Easter Monday, 1916

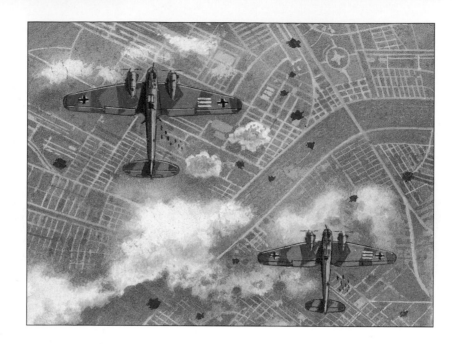

WHAT WAS THE BATTLE OF BRITAIN?

During World War II, the Allied forces of Britain and France became trapped by the rapid German invasion. In June 1940, the French signed a truce with Germany and Britain stood alone against the Germans.

Italy joined the war, siding with the Germans. In June 1940 Hitler made plans to invade Britain. However, he first needed to gain control of the skies. The Battle of Britain began in July 1940 between the German airforce, the Luftwaffe, and Britain's Royal Air Force (RAF). By May 1941 the RAF had gained the upper hand and Hitler stopped the bombing.

FACT FILE

Allied troops wait on a beach at Dunkerque, in northern France, in June 1940. A rescue fleet of naval ships, fishing boats, yachts and ferries sailed across the English Channel from England to carry them back to safety. In all, 300,000 soldiers were rescued.

WHAT WAS THE HOLOCAUST?

Jews held in a concentration camp

In the early 1930s, the Nazi party rose to power in Germany, led by Adolf Hitler. He set up a secret police force, banned opposing political parties and started to persecute minority groups in the German population, such as gypsies and Jews.

During World War II, concentration camps such as Belsen and Auschwitz were set up by the Nazis. Millions of Jews were imprisoned and murdered in these camps because Hitler believed they were responsible for the downfall of Germany. An estimated 6,000,000 Jews died in these camps in World War II, an event known as the Holocaust.

FACT FILE

The official flag of the United Nations consists of a map of the world circled by two olive branches. The olive branches are a symbol of peace.

WHAT WAS THE BLITZKRIEG?

World War II was very different to the first international conflict. Trench warfare, which had claimed so many lives, was now an outdated concept. When Adolf Hitler invaded Poland in September 1939, he unleashed a new and frightening brand of warfare into the world – called 'Blitzkrieg' or lightning war.

The key to the success of Blitzkrieg was the use of tanks in very large numbers and innovative style. The tanks charged ahead independent of the troops and wreaked havoc among defenders. Bursting through defensive lines they created confusion and smashed supply lines.

FACT FILE

World War I had deadly new weaponry as well. The introduction of machine guns changed the way that they fought from the trenches. They could now easily wipe out large numbers of attacking soldiers.

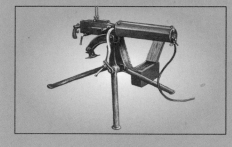

Tanks used during Blitzkrieg

WHAT IS COMMUNISM?

FACT FILE

Chairman Mao and his supporters accused many people of failing to follow communist ideals. Students and young people formed groups of 'Red Guards' in support of Mao.

Communism is a system of political and economic organization in which property is owned by the state and all citizens share the common wealth, more or less according to their needs. After years of civil war, much of China was in ruins. Mao Zedong set about reforming the country according to communist ideals. Land was seized from landowners and divided up among the peasants. In Mao's 'Five-Year Plan' (1953 to 1957) new roads and railways were built, industry boosted, and health and education improved. Mao printed his ideals about his communist state in what became known as Mao's 'Little Red Book', which was read by millions of Chinese.

WHAT WAS THE CUBAN MISSILE CRISIS?

In 1949, the Western Allies formed the North Atlantic Treaty Organization (NATO) for defence against the communist presence in Europe. In the same year, the USSR exploded its first atomic bomb. With both superpowers holding nuclear weapons, fear and mistrust between the two sides increased. The Soviets constructed a wall across Berlin in 1961, separating East from West in the city. In 1962, the Cuban crisis erupted when the USA discovered that the USSR was building missile sites on the island of Cuba in the Caribbean. These sites were within range to launch an attack by nuclear weapons on American cities. The two superpowers came to the brink of war before the USSR agreed to withdraw the weapons.

Although the two superpowers never became involved in direct warfare, both sides became involved in wars elsewhere in the world. The USA fought communism and the USSR helped communist fighters.

The Vietnam War between North and South Vietnam lasted from 1957 until 1976. This is a statue of remembrance in Washington D.C.

FACT FILE

John Fitzgerald Kennedy was US president from 1961 until he was assassinated in 1963. During his presidency the Berlin Wall was built, dividing the city in two and stopping East Germans escaping communist rule.

When?

WHEN WAS THE STONE AGE? 230
WHEN DID THE VIKINGS PROGRESS THROUGH EUROPE? 231

WHEN WAS THE SLAVE TRADE ABOLISHED IN AFRICA? 232
WHEN WERE THE OPIUM WARS? 233

WHEN WAS THE RUSSIAN REVOLUTION? 234
WHEN DID SETTLERS FIRST ARRIVE IN JAPAN? 235

WHEN WAS THE WALL STREET CRASH? 236
WHEN WAS THE RISE OF FASCISM IN EUROPE? 237

WHEN WAS THE FIRST ATOMIC BOMB EXPLOSION? 238
WHEN DID INDIA GAIN INDEPENDENCE? 239

WHEN WAS HONEY FIRST USED? 240
WHEN WAS THE INTERNAL COMBUSTION ENGINE DEVELOPED? 241

WHEN WERE THE FIRST HOUSES BUILT? 242
WHEN WAS THE SHANG DYNASTY? 243

WHEN WERE WEDDING RINGS FIRST WORN? 244

WHEN WAS THE STONE AGE?

Stone Age man (known as Neanderthal man) lived in Europe from about 100,000 to 35,000 years ago. They sheltered in caves, made fire and hunted animals using stone tools and wooden spears.

Historians call this period of prehistory the Stone Age, because stone was the most important material used by the first tool-makers. These early stone-crafting techniques show surprising skill. They chipped or flaked off bits of stone to make shaped tools including hand axes and knives. Both the hand axe and scraper were usually made from flint, while spear heads were often shaped from wood or deer antlers.

The Stone Age hunters killed deer and other animals with spears, bows and stones, often ambushing them on the move. Although they were not as fast as the animals they hunted, they made up for it by using teamwork and accuracy with their weapons.

A skull of a Neanderthal man

Spear head

Scraper

Hand axe

FACT FILE

Stone Age people hunted with bows, spears and flint axes. On the American grasslands, groups of hunters drove to extinction large grazing animals such as mastodons and giant bison.

Ships lie beside a Viking town

WHEN DID THE VIKINGS PROGRESS THROUGH EUROPE?

The Vikings came from Scandinavia (Norway, Denmark and Sweden). Their homelands offered little spare farmland for a growing population, so many Vikings went abroad in search of new lands. The Vikings were farmers, but also fierce warriors, and their first impact on western Europe was a violent one. They began to sail across the North Sea in the late AD 700s, raiding the coasts of Britain and mainland Europe. They raided churches and towns, carrying off loot and slaves. Their raids caused panic, and rulers tried to buy off the invaders with gold. This, however, only encouraged the Vikings to come back for more.

FACT FILE

Decorative brooches such as this were used by both Viking men and women to hold their outer garments (cloaks and tunics) in place.

WHEN WAS THE SLAVE TRADE ABOLISHED IN AFRICA?

During the 1700s the slave trade brought misery to thousands of Africans, who were transported across the Atlantic Ocean and forced to work as slaves on plantations in the Americas. This trade also brought huge wealth to those who ran it – the shipbuilders, shipowners, merchants and traders.

Many people began to condemn the slave trade and to call for it to be abolished. The slave trade came to an end in the British Empire in 1807 and was finally abolished within the empire in 1833. Slavery continued elsewhere, however. It did not come to an end in the United States until after the American Civil War in 1865, and continued in Brazil until 1889.

In 1788 an association was formed in London to encourage British exploration and trade in Africa. Many British explorers set out to explore Africa along its rivers. Probably the most famous of all the expeditions was led by David Livingstone, who set out to look for the source of the River Nile. After being out of contact for almost three years, he was eventually found by the American journalist Henry Stanley.

David Livingstone

A typical colonists' hat

FACT FILE

The anti-slavery movement was strongest in Britain and the USA. Many abolitionists joined the struggle for rights for black people.

WHEN WERE THE OPIUM WARS?

The Manchus ruled China for more than 250 years, from 1644 until 1912. This time is known as the Qing dynasty. In the early 1800s, British merchants started to trade opium illegally from India to China. Despite the fact that the addictive dangers of opium were well known, the British government backed the merchants. They wanted to force China to accept more open trade.

The first Opium War broke out in 1839, and was started when Chinese officials seized 20,000 chests of opium in Guangzhou. It ended with the Treaty of Nanjing in 1842. Under the terms of this treaty, Hong Kong became a British colony and more Chinese ports were opened up to European trade. A second Opium War (1856 to 1860) extended the trading rights of European nations in China. Under Manchu rule, all Chinese males had to follow the tradition of wearing their hair in a pigtail. It was seen as a sign of loyalty to the Qing dynasty.

FACT FILE

The skyline of modern Hong Kong. The island of Hong Kong came under British control in 1842, and Britain later gained part of the nearby Kowloon Peninsula. Control of Hong Kong passed back to the Chinese government in 1997.

WHEN WAS THE RUSSIAN REVOLUTION?

The last tsar, Nicholas II, ruled from 1894 until his abdication in 1917. In the early years of his reign there was increasing discontent amongst ordinary Russians. Many people, including the Bolshevik leader Vladimir Illyich Lenin, followed the teachings of Karl Marx, the founder of communism. In 1905 this discontent boiled over when troops fired on thousands of striking workers outside the tsar's Winter Palace in St Petersburg. The rebellion was quickly put down, but hundreds of workers were killed and wounded.

In early 1917 riots broke out again and this time the troops supported the rioters. Nicholas II abdicated, and a provisional government was put in place.

FACT FILE

Nicholas II and his family. Imprisoned by the Bolsheviks in 1917, they were most probably shot the following year.

WHEN DID SETTLERS FIRST ARRIVE IN JAPAN?

People from mainland Asia had settled on the islands of Japan by 7000 BC. The original inhabitants may have been the Ainu, about 15,000 of whom still live in Japan. The early Japanese lived by hunting and fishing. Farming began around 1000 to 500 BC, when the Japanese learned to grow rice, a skill brought over from China. They also began to make metal tools and to make pottery using a potter's wheel. The site in Tokyo where pottery was first found, gives this period of history its name – Yayoi.

The Yayoi farmers dug ditches to irrigate their rice fields. They built thatched homes and storehouses on stilts for their rice crop. Farmers lived together in villages, and each village was led by a chief who was often a woman shaman, or magician. The women shamans of Japan were extremely powerful figures.

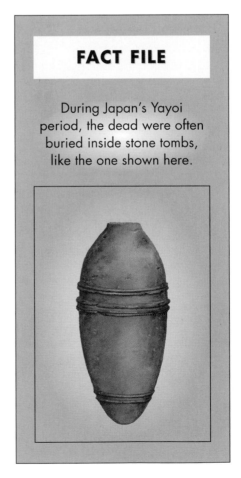

FACT FILE

During Japan's Yayoi period, the dead were often buried inside stone tombs, like the one shown here.

WHEN WAS THE WALL STREET CRASH?

In the late 1920s, the price of shares on the New York Stock Exchange increased rapidly. More and more people bought stocks and shares in the hope of selling them again when their price had gone up – therefore making a large profit. When prices dropped in October 1929, people rushed to sell their stocks and shares before it was too late, but prices fell even further. This event is known as the Wall Street Crash. Thousands of people lost all their money, many businesses and banks shut down and unemployment soared.

FACT FILE

During the worst years of the Depression, many people were forced to rely on charity and government hand-outs for their most basic needs. In 1932 Franklin D. Roosevelt was elected US present. His 'New Deal' aimed to create jobs and to protect people's savings by regulating banks more closely.

The Stock Exchange at the time of the collapse

WHEN WAS THE RISE OF
FASCISM IN EUROPE?

Many people hoped that World War I was the 'war to end all wars'. However, during the 1920s and 1930s there were a lot of political changes in many countries. In 1922 these changes led to the growth of the Fascist movement. The word 'Fascism' from *fasces*, meaning a bundle of branches. Fascism promised strong leadership and to restore the national economy and pride. This was a very powerful message in the years of the Great Depression, and many people in Europe supported the various Fascist parties.

   Italy was the first country to have a Fascist ruler. In 1922, Benito Mussolini marched to Rome and demanded that the Italian king, Victor Emmanuel III, make him Prime Minister.

FACT FILE

Sir Oswald Mosley knew Adolf Hitler through his wife, Diana Mitford. He was violently opposed to postwar 'non-white' immigration.

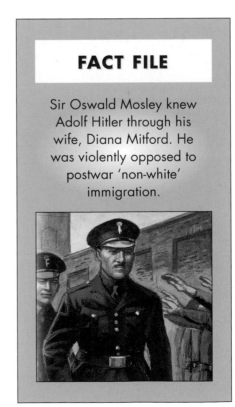

WHEN WAS THE FIRST ATOMIC BOMB EXPLOSION?

Technological advances in the machines and weapons of war were rapid during the 20th century. During World War I, inventions included the tank and the fighter aircraft. At sea, one of the major advances in military marine technology happened before the war, with the building of the battleship *Dreadnought*.

During World War II, the Germans used a new type of warfare, known as *Blitzkreig* (lightning war). But even more horrifying was the invention of the atomic bomb in the United States.

The first atomic bomb was exploded in an experiment in New Mexico, USA in July 1945. Only a month later, atomic bombs were

used to end the war. The bombs dropped on Japan killed about 130,000 people. Many more suffered terrible after effects such as radiation and burn injuries. It was this terrifying bomb that was used to bring the war against Japan to its catastrophic end.

FACT FILE

Both the British and the French armies experimented with tanks during World War I. These armoured vehicles were first used to effect at the battle of Cambrai in 1917.

WHEN DID INDIA GAIN INDEPENDENCE?

FACT FILE

Mohandas Gandhi was known as Mahatma Gandhi. He was assassinated in 1948, at the end of India's long struggle for independence.

Many Indians wanted independence from British rule, and a chance to build up industry and wealth in India itself. By the end of World War II it was clear that Britain could no longer ignore the demands of the Indian people. But negotiations were complicated by the demands of Muslims in India. Violence broke out between Hindus and Muslims, and Indians and British leaders eventually agreed to divide India into the two states of Hindu India and Muslim Pakistan.

India gained its independence in August 1947. Millions of Hindus and Muslims fled from their homes. As people tried to move to their new homes, hundreds of thousands of people were killed.

WHEN WAS HONEY FIRST USED?

Honey has been used as a sweetener since very ancient times, since, apart from dates, it was practically the only way early man could get sugar. It is mentioned in the Bible, the Koran and Homer, as well as many other Greek writers.

It is recorded as being used as a medicine in Egypt, as well as in embalming fluid and as a paste for cosmetics, such as the black kohl they used around their eyes. It was used throughout history to make a sweet, and very strong, beer called 'mead', and to sweeten wine. In ancient India, it was used to preserve and sweeten foods.

Scientists have not yet managed to recreate honey in the laboratory, and there have been concerns about future supplies of honey worldwide because of a parasitic mite called Varroa, which preys upon the bees until the hive dies, as well as the northwards sweep of killer bees in southern North America and aggressive, and less productive African bees in Europe.

FACT FILE

Honey bees tell other worker bees in the colony where good sources of food can be found, by performing a special dance, called the honey dance, on their return to the hive.

WHEN WAS THE INTERNAL COMBUSTION ENGINE DEVELOPED?

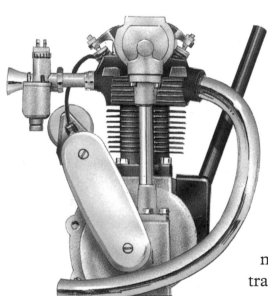

Though best known for his invention of the diesel engine, the French-born Rudolf Diesel was also an eminent thermal engineer, a connoisseur of the arts, a linguist, and a social theorist. During 1885 Diesel set up his first shop-laboratory in Paris and began his 13-year ordeal of creating his distinctive engine. At Augsburg, on August 10, 1893, Diesel's first model, a single 10-foot (3m) iron cylinder with a flywheel at its base, ran on its own power for the first time. Diesel spent two more years on improvements and on the last day of 1896 demonstrated another model with the spectacular mechanical efficiency of 75.6 percent. His engines were used to power pipelines, electric and water plants, automobiles, trucks and marine craft. It was also later used in applications including mines, oil fields, factories, and transoceanic shipping.

FACT FILE

Diesel originally conceived the combustion engine as an alternative to the oversized, expensive, fuel-wasting steam engine, which was being widely used in industry.

WHEN WERE THE FIRST HOUSES BUILT?

FACT FILE

Ice Age hunters made shelters from the bones of mammoths. They made the framework of bones and filled in the gaps with skins, turf and moss.

Many early people took refuge in caves, but as they spread out through regions where there were none, they had to find alternatives. Hunters would have made tents from animal skins, while other people made huts from interwoven twigs and plastered mud in the gaps to keep the wind out, and straw on the roof to stop the rain.

The ancient Egyptians are believed to have been among the first to make sun-dried mud bricks, while in Mesopotamia people developed a way of making bricks stronger and more long-lasting, by placing them in a hot fire and firing them. At places like Babylon, such bricks have lasted for thousands of years.

WHEN WAS THE SHANG DYNASTY?

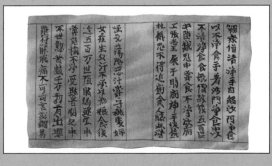

Shang food vessel

The Shang dynasty was the earliest known Chinese family of rulers. The dynasty governed from the sixteenth to eleventh centuries BC.

Its central point was in what is now known as the northern Henan Province, in the valley of the Huang He (the Yellow River). Shang society was based on agriculture, but because of their perfection of irrigation techniques the kings became wealthy and a tradition of beautiful bronze work grew up. As well as decorative vessels, they used bronze for chariot fixtures and a wide variety of weapons. Most Shang relics came from Anyang, a Shang capital, which had royal palaces, houses, temples and elaborate tombs. Beautiful marble and jade carvings have also been found by archaeologists.

FACT FILE

The Shang scribes perfected the early form of the Chinese alphabet. Their version had more than 3,000 symbols.

WHEN WERE WEDDING RINGS FIRST WORN?

The tradition of a bride wearing a wedding ring goes back so far that its origins are obscure.

We know the Egyptians wore wedding rings. In hieroglyphics, a circle is the symbol of eternity, so a wedding ring indicated an unending and indivisible bond. The wedding ring makes its first appearance in Christianity in about AD 900.

Some people see a more sinister history to the wedding ring and believe that it is a diminutive version of the slave band bracelet or neck collar that captive women wore in prehistoric times to indicate that they were someone's property. Now, the wearing of wedding rings is practised in almost all cultures, often by men as well as women.

Gold is the traditional metal for wedding rings because it does not tarnish and so is also a symbol of the hoped-for everlasting marriage.

FACT FILE

In most cultures, the ring is worn on the fourth finger of the left hand, supposedly because the ancient Greeks believed that a vein passed from this finger directly to the heart. However, it is more likely that it is simply because the fourth finger of the left hand is not used very much.

Where?

WHERE DOES THE WORD 'HISTORY' COME FROM? 246
WHERE WOULD YOU SEE A HOME OF MAMMOTH BONES? 247

WHERE ARE THE RUINS OF PERSEPOLIS? 248
WHERE DOES THE NAME 'DRUID' COME FROM? 249

WHERE WAS ETRURIA? 250
WHERE WERE THE FIRST GLADIATOR GAMES HELD? 251

WHERE WAS THE SILK ROAD? 252
WHERE WAS THE BIGGEST GROWTH OF THE MUSLIM EMPIRE? 253

WHERE WAS THE BATTLE OF CRECY? 254
WHERE ARE THE FORBIDDEN AND IMPERIAL CITIES? 255

WHERE DID THE CRUSADES TAKE PLACE? 256
WHERE DID WILLIAM BUILD NORMAN CASTLES? 257

WHERE DID THE 'SALT MARCH' TAKE PLACE? 258
WHERE WAS THE BATTLE OF DIEN BIEN PHU? 259

WHERE DOES THE WORD 'HISTORY' COME FROM?

History comes from a Greek word meaning 'what is known by asking'. The job of a historian is to ask questions and make sense of the answers.

The Greeks were among the first people to write history based on first-hand reporting of the facts. Herodotus (who died in 425 BC) wrote about the wars between the Greeks and the Persians. He travelled and talked to people who had taken part in the wars.

Historians work from a viewpoint. The first people to write their own history were the Chinese. We know the name of one early Chinese historian, Sima Qian, who wrote a history of China in about 100 BC. Early historians felt it was important to write down the stories and legends of the past,

FACT FILE

The word 'archaeology' comes from two Greek words and means 'the study of old things'. Many archaeological discoveries are made by digging in the ground at sites where ancient people lived.

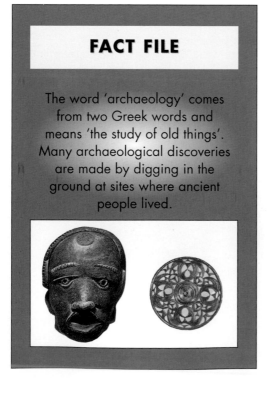

and show how their state had come into existence. Sometimes people who made history also wrote about it. Julius Caesar, the Roman general, wrote his own book about his campaigns in Gaul.

WHERE WOULD YOU SEE A HOME OF MAMMOTH BONES?

Around 18,000 years ago, the last of a series of Ice Ages gripped much of the Northern Hemisphere. Icecaps spread southwards across Europe and North America. The sea level fell, uncovering land bridges, which animals and people crossed – between Asia and Alaska for example.

Ice Age hunters, clothed only in animal skins, adapted to living in these freezing conditions. They built shelters from the bones of mammoths. They made the framework from bones and filled in the gaps with skins, turf and moss. Groups of men drove the animals into swamps, where they became trapped and were killed with spears or rocks.

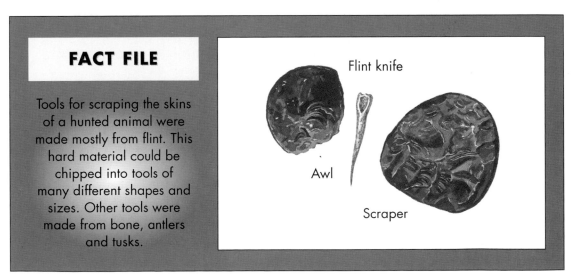

FACT FILE

Tools for scraping the skins of a hunted animal were made mostly from flint. This hard material could be chipped into tools of many different shapes and sizes. Other tools were made from bone, antlers and tusks.

Flint knife

Awl

Scraper

WHERE ARE THE RUINS OF PERSEPOLIS?

FACT FILE

Ten thousand soldiers called the Immortals formed the core of the Persian army. Each spearman or archer was instantly replaced if killed.

Persepolis lies in the southwest of what is now Iran, in a strategic position in the mountains. It was built as one of his capitals by King Darius I of Persia in around 500 BC. Large stone and mud-brick palaces were built and the city became the royal ceremonial area for the New Year's religious rituals, when Darius and his successors would renew their divine rights as kings, and expect gifts from all the client kings of the empire.

In 330 BC, having already defeated the last Persian king, another Darius, Alexander the Great seized Persepolis and the city's life came to an end. Archaeologists have uncovered many of the ruins. Some of these ruins have been restored and visitors are able to see around some of the buildings of the kings' great palace.

WHERE DOES THE NAME 'DRUID' COME FROM?

The name 'Druid' is derived from 'oak'. *Dru-wid* combines the word roots 'oak' and 'knowledge'. It was Pliny the Elder in his *Naturalis Historia* (XVI 95), who associated the Druids with mistletoe and oak groves:

> 'The Druids . . . hold nothing more sacred than the mistletoe and the tree on which it grows provided it is an oak. They choose the oak to form groves, and they do not perform any religious rites without its foliage . . .'

Celtic priests, also known as Druids, have often been identified as wizards and soothsayers. They performed mysterious rites in sacred groves of trees. The Moon, the oak and mistletoe were all magical to the Druids, and so too were many animals. However, in pre-Christian Celtic society they formed an intellectual class comprising philosophers, judges, educators, historians, doctors, seers, astronomers and astrologers. The earliest surviving classical references to Druids date to the second century BC.

FACT FILE

Around the campfire at night, Celtic poets, storytellers and musicians would pass on tales of the gods and of events in the history of the Celtic people.

WHERE WAS ETRURIA?

Etruria was an area of Italy, known today as Tuscany, Umbria and Latium. Etruria originally extended from the Arno in the north to the Tiber in the south, and from the Apennines in the east to the Tyrrhenian Sea in the west. Their origins are unclear. They were a highly organized, militaristic society, and rapidly extended their territories north across the Apennines into the Po Valley and south across the Tiber River into Latium and Campania. The civilization reached its height in the 400s BC, although the Etruscans lost control of Rome in 510 BC when the last Etruscan king, Tarquinius Superbus, was driven out, leaving Rome a republic. Rome is thought to have obtained many of her military techniques from the Etruscans as well as such customs as slavery.

FACT FILE

Part of a carved stone relief depicting a Roman funeral procession. The pallbearers carried the dead person on a raised bier, followed by the mourners.

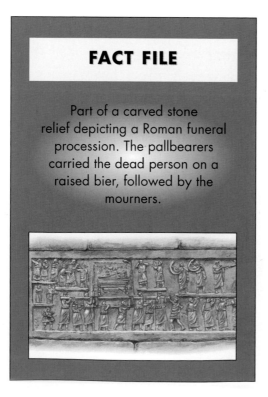

WHERE WERE THE FIRST GLADIATOR GAMES HELD?

Records state that the first gladiator games were held to commemorate the funeral of a Roman aristocrat in a cattle market in 264 BC. There were many venues for fights, but the most famous one, the Colosseum in Rome was built between AD 72 to 81 by the emperor Vespasian. There, wild beasts fought in the morning and the gladiators fought in the afternoon.

Gladiators were highly trained, and fought using many different types of weapons – a shield and sword, a net and long trident, for example. They usually fought until one was killed, but the life of the loser could be spared if the spectators waved handkerchiefs, or the emperor gave him the thumbs-up, rather than the thumbs-down.

FACT FILE

Most gladiators were prisoners of war, slaves or criminals. Slaves wore tags advertising their skills and good character to enhance their price at auction.

WHERE WAS THE SILK ROAD?

The Silk Road was a group of ancient trade routes that connected China and Europe, but was a concept rather than a physical road and flourished primarily from 100 BC to AD 1500. The routes stretched across about 5, 000 miles (8,050 km) from the Mediterranean, across Arabia, through India and what is now Burma to the far edge of China.

The Silk Road was named after the vast amounts of Chinese silk carried along it, but parts of it had been trade routes for thousands of years before. Towns and cities sprang up along the route to provide facilities for food, water and recreation, as well as goods for trade. This trade made a number of countries very rich, as the merchants had to pass through to avoid being attacked by bandits. Other goods included gold, spices and jewellery. Camel caravans carried most goods across the dry, harsh regions along the Silk Road.

By AD 800, with the Ottoman empire in turmoil, traffic fell as traders started to travel by safer sea routes.

FACT FILE

The Chinese were the first to learn to make silk, and they guarded their secret. They had a monopoly until the 500s AD, when a merchant is thought to have smuggled some silk worms back in a hollow cane.

WHERE WAS THE BIGGEST GROWTH OF THE MUSLIM EMPIRE?

The advance of Islam seemed unstoppable in the late 600s. The Byzantine and Persian empires could not halt the armies of Islam, and nor could Egypt. By AD 700 Muslims controlled most of the North African coast, and ships patrolled the Mediterranean Sea and Indian Ocean. Muslims from Morocco invaded Spain, but the advance of Islam into western Europe was stopped in AD 732 by the Frankish army of Charles Martel. Under the Ummayad family rule there were four classes of citizens: Arabian Muslims; new converts; Christians, Jews and Mandaens (a Persian sect); and slaves. The new converts included people from Egypt, Syria, Persia and Asia Minor. They adopted Arab ways, but brought to the Arabs a wealth of new learning in philosophy, medicine, art and science.

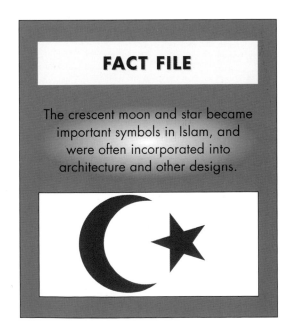

FACT FILE

The crescent moon and star became important symbols in Islam, and were often incorporated into architecture and other designs.

WHERE WAS THE BATTLE OF CRÉCY?

The Battle of Crécy was the first important battle of the Hundred Years War (1337 to 1453) at the site of the present village of Crécy, in northern France. The Hundred Years War began in 1337 and continued periodically for more than a century.

In this battle, English archers on foot, under Edward III, defeated Philip VI's much larger force of mounted knights. More than 1,000 were killed, as was almost half of the French force in the Battle of Crécy. The hero of the battle was Edward, the Black Prince, son of Edward III of England.

FACT FILE

Knights decorated their shield or standard with the heraldic symbols of their own coat of arms. This made it easier to identify the knight in full armour. Each coat of arms had its own unique design.

WHERE ARE THE FORBIDDEN AND IMPERIAL CITIES?

The Forbidden City and the Imperial City lie within the Inner City, an area in Beijing, the capital of China. The Forbidden City includes palaces of former Chinese emperors. It was so named because only the emperor's household was allowed to enter it.

The buildings in this part of Beijing are now preserved as museums. The Imperial City surrounds the Forbidden City. It includes lakes, parks and the residences of China's Communist leaders. The Gate of Heavenly Peace stands at the southern edge of the Imperial City, overlooking Tiananmen Square.

FACT FILE

The first Ming emperor Chu Yuan-Chang turned Beijing into one of the greatest cities in the world, with the Forbidden City at its core.

WHERE DID THE CRUSADES TAKE PLACE?

FACT FILE

The word crusade comes from the Latin word crux, meaning cross. 'To take up the cross' meant to become a crusader.

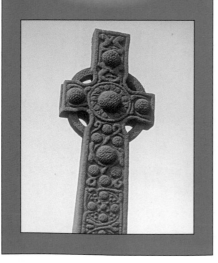

Crusades were the military expeditions organized mainly to recapture Palestine during the Middle Ages. Palestine, also called the Holy Land, was important to Christians because it was the region where Jesus Christ had lived. Palestine lay along the eastern coast of the Mediterranean Sea and Muslims had taken control of it from the Christians. The crusaders, who came from Western Europe, organized eight major expeditions between AD 1096 and 1270. This was a period when Western Europe was expanding its economy and increasing its military forces. Kings, nobles and thousands of knights, peasants and townspeople took part in the Crusades. They had two main goals: first to gain permanent control of the Holy Land and second to protect the Byzantine empire.

WHERE DID WILLIAM BUILD NORMAN CASTLES?

Conwy castle

FACT FILE

The Bayeux Tapestry was made by the Normans to celebrate their victory over the English in 1066. It is a huge series of pictures depicting incidents during the conquest.

The introduction of castles to England followed the Norman conquest of 1066. In fact, castles were the means by which William the Conqueror and his followers secured their hold on England following their victory at the battle of Hastings. William ordered castles to be built at Warwick, Nottingham, York, Lincoln, Cambridge and Huntingdon. These defensive structures helped to secure his newly acquired lands. The first Norman castles were hurriedly constructed of earth and timber.

Conwy castle, in north Wales, is typical of the castles built by the Normans to withstand a long siege. Windsor Castle, Berkshire, is perhaps England's most famous castle.

WHERE DID THE 'SALT MARCH' TAKE PLACE?

Mohandas Gandhi (1869 to 1948), known as Mahatma Gandhi, was the father of the Indian nation. He helped to free India from British control by a unique method of non-violent resistance. He is still revered as one of the foremost spiritual and political leaders of the twentieth century.

Gandhi believed that non-violence was a more effective way to get his message heard than violence, and in 1930 protested against the British government's monopoly on salt – possessing salt not bought from the government was a criminal offence – by leading his followers on a 240-mile (386-km) march to the coast, where they made salt from seawater. Gandhi spent seven years in prison in total because of his protests against British injustice, and lived to see independence in 1947.

FACT FILE

In the middle of the Indian flag is an ancient symbol of a wheel. It is known as the Dharma Chakra, which means the 'Wheel of Law'. India gained her independence from Britain on August 15, 1947.

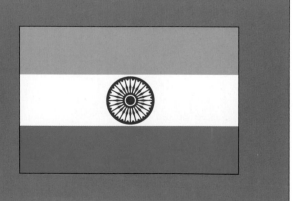

WHERE WAS THE BATTLE OF DIEN BIEN PHU?

Vietnam is a tropical country in southeast Asia. China governed the area from about 100 BC until AD 900, when the Vietnamese established an independent state. Fighting broke out between French forces and the Viet Minh in 1946. It ended in 1954, with the French defeat in the Battle of Dien Bien Phu. An international conference to arrange a peace settlement also took place at this time. In 1957, Viet Minh members in the South began to rebel against the South Vietnamese government. Fighting broke out and it developed into the Vietnam War. The United States became the ally of the South.

FACT FILE

The Vietnam War showed for the first time how a small country like North Vietnam could take on and eventually defeat the military might of the US, by using superior tactics.

Science & Technology

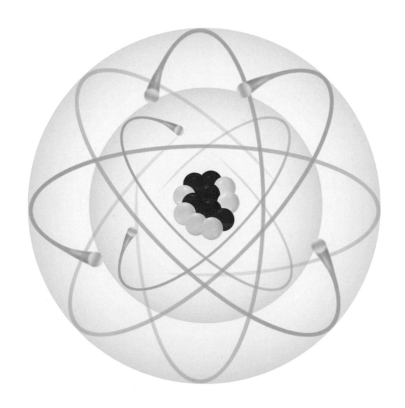

The Earth

WHEN IS SUMMER SOLSTICE? 262
WHEN IS THE SHORTEST DAY? 263

WHY DO EARTHQUAKES OCCUR? 264
WHAT IS A SEISMOGRAPH? 265

HOW ARE MOUNTAINS FORMED? 266
WHEN WAS THE TOP OF EVEREST FIRST REACHED? 267

WHY DOES WATER BECOME SALTY? 268
WHEN WAS THE LONGEST DROUGHT? 269

HOW MANY PARTS DOES THE EARTH CONSIST OF? 270
WHAT WAS PANGAEA? 271

HOW DO GEYSERS GET SO HOT? 272
WHEN DO WE SEE THE SPECTRUM OF LIGHT? 273

WHAT IS GRAVITY? 274
WHEN DOES LIGHTNING STRIKE? 275

WHEN WAS LIGHTNING FIRST UNDERSTOOD? 276

WHEN IS SUMMER SOLSTICE?

The Earth revolves around the Sun and at the same time it revolves on its own axis. As it moves around the Sun, it is also spinning like a top. If the axis of the Earth were at right angles to the path of the Earth around the Sun, all the days of the year would be the same length. However, the Earth is tilted at an angle of 66.5°. In June, the northern hemisphere is tilted towards the Sun and it receives more sunshine during a day. This is its warmest season called summer. On the 21 June, the Sun is directly over the Tropic of Cancer and it is midsummer in the northern hemisphere. This is the time known as the summer solstice.

FACT FILE

The Sun is the source of light and heat for the solar system. The four planets closest to the Sun are small and solid, the closest being Mercury. An asteroid belt separates these from the four larger planets, which are made up of gas.

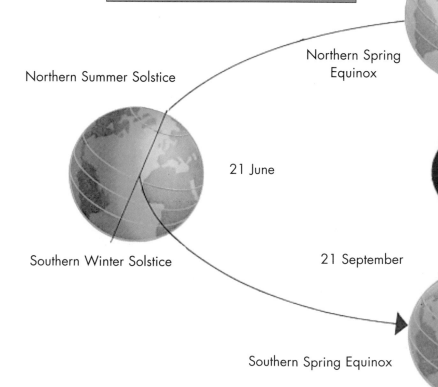

Northern Summer Solstice

Northern Spring Equinox

21 June

Southern Winter Solstice

21 September

Southern Spring Equinox

WHEN IS THE SHORTEST DAY?

FACT FILE

Mars is known as the 'Red Planet' because it is covered by a stone desert containing lots of iron oxide, making it appear red. The water and oxygen that used to exist on Mars are now locked up in these iron deposits, so the planet has hardly any atmosphere.

The shortest day of the year is in the winter solstice, which is 21 December. When the northern hemisphere is turned toward the Sun, the countries north of the equator have their summer season, and the countries south of the equator have their winter season. When the direct rays of the Sun fall on the southern hemisphere, it is their summer and it is winter in the northern hemisphere. There are two days in the year when night and day are equal all over the world. They come in the spring and fall, just halfway between the two solstices. One is the autumnal equinox in September, and the other is the spring equinox in March.

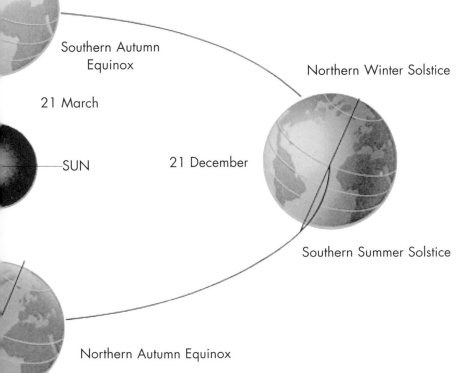

Southern Autumn Equinox

21 March

Northern Winter Solstice

SUN

21 December

Southern Summer Solstice

Northern Autumn Equinox

WHY DO EARTHQUAKES OCCUR?

Our planet is a very restless place. Every 30 seconds, the ground suddenly rumbles and trembles. Most of the movements are so slight that they are not felt. Others can be so large they cause complete disaster. Big cracks appear in the land, streets buckle and buildings simply crumble. In fact, whole towns and cities can be destroyed. These are called earthquakes and the reason they occur is because the Earth's crust is made up of moving parts called plates. When these plates slide past or into each other, the rocks jolt and send out shock waves.

FACT FILE

Both mining and tunnelling operations are known to have caused earthquakes in areas that are already under tension due to movements in the Earth's crust.

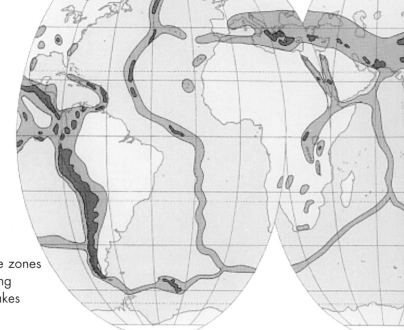

 Major earthquake zones
Areas experiencing frequent earthquakes

WHAT IS A SEISMOGRAPH?

FACT FILE

The edges of the Pacific plate are surrounded by earthquakes, volcanic activity and hot springs, caused by the crust shifts and hot lava rising near the surface.

From time to time we hear news of a big earthquake that has taken place somewhere far away, and although we don't usually feel the Earth shaking, scientists can make an exact record of the earthquake from anywhere in the world. This is with instruments called seismographs, the study of earthquakes being known as seismology. The seismograph picks up the signals, which are caused by one rock mass rubbing against the other with such ferocity that the energy produced causes vibrations in the rocks, vibrations that can travel thousands of miles and still be felt.

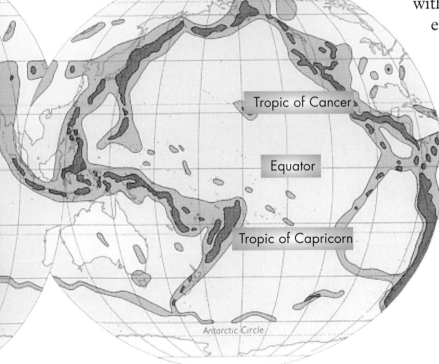

Arctic Circle

Tropic of Cancer

Equator

Tropic of Capricorn

Antarctic Circle

HOW ARE MOUNTAINS FORMED?

Mountains can be formed in three different ways. Volcanoes form mountains when lava from deep inside the Earth cools and hardens on the surface.

Other mountains are formed when two plates move towards each other under pressure, or where an oceanic plate is pushed under a continental crust. The pressure causes the ground near the joining plate margins to fault and fold. The ground is forced upwards to form mountains. The Rockies, Alps, Andes, Urals and Himalayas were all formed in this way.

Finally, the Earth's crust can fracture and create faults, which means that large blocks of land can be moved upwards or downwards. Faults in the rocks normally occur when there is a lot of pressure on the rocks. Mountain building is a slow process and happens over centuries.

FACT FILE

Rockslides are common where forests have been destroyed on mountainsides. There are no longer any tree roots to stabilize the loose material.

Three ways in which a mountain can form

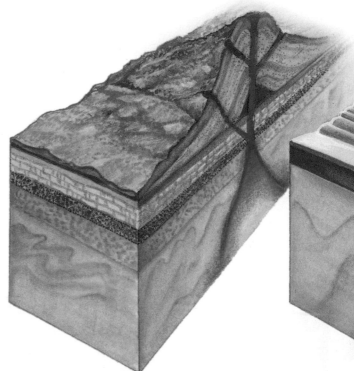

Volcano

WHEN WAS THE TOP OF EVEREST FIRST REACHED?

FACT FILE

Mountain peaks are often seen to be surrounded by layers of cloud. This is because as winds laden with water are blown towards the mountains, they are forced to rise and the temperature drops. The water condenses into clouds at these higher altitudes.

Mount Everest, which is in the Himalayas, is 29,000 feet (8,863m) high. At these altitudes, mountains are always covered in snow and ice, and there is little oxygen to breathe. Mount Everest was finally conquered on May 29, 1953, when a Nepalese guide, Tenzing Norgay, and a New Zealander, Edmund Hillary, reached the highest point on the Earth's surface. Since then, many people have climbed Everest, and all the world's major peaks have now been conquered.

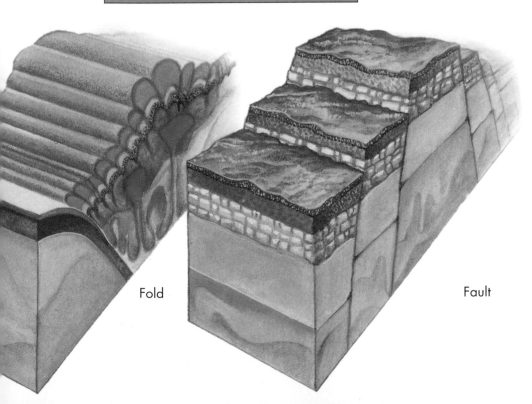

Fold

Fault

WHY DOES WATER BECOME SALTY?

FACT FILE

Lighthouses were built to warn ships at sea that they were approaching land and rocky water. Their beam of light across the waves made travelling by boat much safer.

Water becomes salty when minerals (including salts) dissolve into it. This process begins when rainwater falls on the land and erodes rock. The minerals in rock are dissolved into the rainwater.

These dissolved minerals in the rainwater enter streams and rivers, gradually working their way into the seas and oceans.

This is a process which is constantly taking place, so the level and concentration of salt in the oceans and seas is always increasing. Some of the minerals are consumed by organisms in the water, but the vast majority of them constitute the saltiness of the water.

WHEN WAS THE LONGEST DROUGHT?

The longest drought in recorded history took place in Calama, in the Atacama desert of Northern Chile. For four centuries, beginning in 1571, no rain fell in the area. It was not until 1971 that rainfall was first recorded again. The Atacama desert, which lies between the Andes and the Pacific ocean, is recognized as the driest place in the world.

The Atacama desert remains so dry because it lies in a region where there is constant high air pressure, with little air movement, and with few clouds overhead.

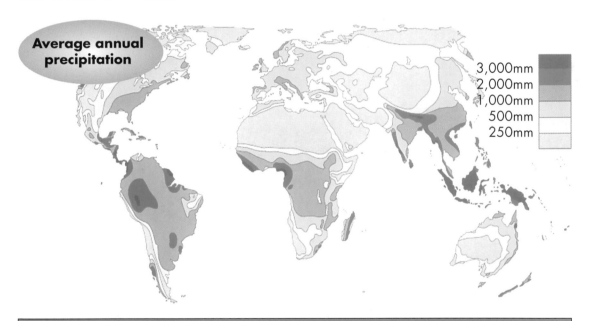

Average annual precipitation

3,000mm
2,000mm
1,000mm
500mm
250mm

FACT FILE

Some people believe that animals are good predictors of weather. One such belief is that if cows are standing in their field, then dry weather is expected. If they are lying down, however, rain is expected.

HOW MANY PARTS DOES THE EARTH CONSIST OF?

The Earth consists of five parts: the first, the atmosphere, is gaseous; the second, the hydrosphere, is liquid; the third, fourth, and fifth, the lithosphere, mantle and core, are largely solid. The atmosphere is the gaseous envelope that surrounds the solid body of the planet. Although it has a thickness of more than 700 miles (1100 km), about half its mass is concentrated in the lower 3.5 miles (5.6 km). The lithosphere, consisting mainly of the cold, rigid, rocky crust of the Earth, extends to depths of 60 miles (100 km). The hydrosphere is the layer of water that, in the form of the oceans, covers approximately 70.8 percent of the surface of the Earth. The mantle and core are the heavy interior of the Earth, making up most of the Earth's mass.

FACT FILE

The Earth's inner core is made up mostly of iron and nickel. It is 850 miles (1,370 km) deep and is thought to have a temperature of around 4,500°C.

WHAT WAS PANGAEA?

Some 225 million years ago all the world's land masses were joined together into one supercontinent, Pangaea, surrounded by a single universal sea, the Panthalassa. Through the upheavals that we have since come to know as plate tectonics, the shifting of the Earth's crust tore the supercontinent apart around the middle of the Mesozoic period and large bodies of land drifted across the surface of the Earth to ultimately become our present-day continents. It is now believed that the several moving plates of the Earth's crust were formed by volcanic activity. The clues to the movement of the Earth's surface can only be found on the present-day continents in rocks, fossils and structures older than about 200 million years.

FACT FILE

Certain species of terrestrial mammals became isolated, as a result, in Antarctica, South America, Africa and Australia. It was thousands of years before volcanic eruption would reunite South and North America in a land bridge.

HOW DO GEYSERS GET SO HOT?

Most of the water in a geyser, which is hot when it comes to the surface, originates from rain and snow which gathers in underground reservoirs, which act like storage basins, connected to the surface by a tube.

The rock further down inside the Earth is extremely hot, and steam-like gasses from the rocks rise up through cracks in the rock, heating the water in the reservoirs to more than boiling point.

When a combination of steam and water rises freely from the depths, a continuously boiling hot spring is created.

Geysers, on the other hand, are created when the tube or passageway is not straight, as is often the case, erupting onto the surface as the water is converted into steam. Because steam needs more space than water, as this eruption takes place it pushes up through the channel of water above it, making an explosive ejection of steam thrusting into the air, causing the spectacular phenomenon of a geyser.

FACT FILE

This hotel heats water for leisure purposes. The pool is a luxury attraction and people have always found pleasure swimming in warm water.

WHEN DO WE SEE THE SPECTRUM OF LIGHT?

Sir Isaac Newton

TELL ME ABOUT SCIENCE & TECHNOLOGY : THE EARTH

FACT FILE

Sir Isaac Newton used his discoveries about light to build a new kind of telescope. It used a reflecting mirror instead of glass lenses to magnify images.

Sir Isaac Newton of Cambridge University first uncovered the secrets of how light is divided up. We think of ordinary light as being 'white', but really light is a mixture of red, orange, yellow, green, blue and violet. When sunlight strikes the bevelled edge of a mirror, or the edge of a glass prism, or the surface of a soap bubble, we can see the different hues in light. What actually happens is that the white light is broken up into the different wave lengths that are seen by our eyes. These wave lengths form a band of parallel stripes, each hue grading into the one next to it. This band is called a 'spectrum'. In a spectrum, the red line is always at one end and the blue and violet lines at the other.

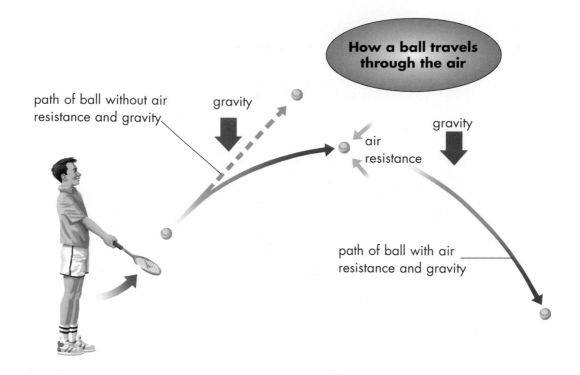

How a ball travels through the air

path of ball without air resistance and gravity

gravity

gravity

air resistance

path of ball with air resistance and gravity

WHAT IS GRAVITY?

Gravity is the force that pulls towards the centre of the Earth. It doesn't matter where you stand on the Earth's surface, the ground is always 'down'.

The force of gravity depends on the mass, or amount of material, of an object. Objects only feel heavy because of their mass.

Newton realised that gravity not only affects the Earth, but it also controls the movement of the planets and the stars, as well as the orbit of the Moon around the Earth. When you whirl something around your head on the end of a piece of string, it flies outwards and appears to defy the force of gravity. This is called centrifugal force. When you let go of the string, the centrifugal force makes the object fly away in a straight line.

FACT FILE

Sir Isaac Newton (1643–1727) was the first scientist to develop the laws of gravity. He supposedly was inspired by seeing an apple fall from a tree.

WHEN DOES LIGHTNING STRIKE?

To understand exactly what lightning is, we must recall a fact we know about electricity. We know that things become electrically charged – either positively or negatively. A positive charge has a great attraction for a negative one. As the charges become greater, this attraction becomes stronger. A point is finally reached where the strain of being kept apart becomes too great for the charges. A discharge takes place to relieve the strain and make the two bodies electrically equal. This is exactly what happens in the case of lightning. This discharge follows the path which offers the least resistance. That is the reason why lightning often zigzags. Moist air is only a fair conductor of electricity, which is why lightning often stops when it starts raining.

FACT FILE

The electrical nature of the nervous system was discovered after Italian scientist Galvani noticed how frogs' legs twitched when an electrical current was applied to the nerve.

WHEN WAS LIGHTNING FIRST UNDERSTOOD?

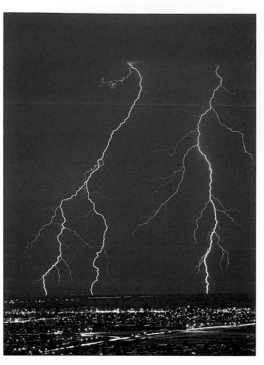

Ben Franklin (1706–1790) was an American with many talents. He was a printer, scientist and politician who played an important part in founding the United States.

He discovered the nature of lightning while flying a kite during a thunderstorm. Franklin noticed sparks jumping from a key tied to the end of the wet string. This could very easily have killed him, but it did not. He went on to invent the lightning conductor, a strip of copper that is run from the top of a building to the ground, in order that lightning can earth itself safely.

Lightning is a significant weather hazard and occurs at an average rate of 50 to 100 discharges per second. Lightning rods and metallic conductors can be used to protect a structure by intercepting and diverting the lightning current into the ground as harmlessly as possible. When lightning is likely to occur, people are advised to stay indoors or in a car, away from open doors and windows and to avoid contact with any electrical appliances or plumbing that might be exposed to the outside environment.

FACT FILE

A lightning conductor is a metal rod that is placed so that it points upwards above the highest point of a tall building. If lightning does strike the building, it is the conductor, not the building itself, that the spark hits.

The Natural World

WHEN DID THE FIRST PLANTS APPEAR? 278
WHEN IS CLIMAX VEGETATION ACHIEVED? 279

WHEN DID DARWIN SAIL TO THE GALAPAGOS ISLANDS? 280
WHEN DID DARWIN PUBLISH *ON THE ORIGIN OF SPECIES*? 281

WHY DID LINNAEUS DEVELOP A CLASSIFICATION SYSTEM? 282
WHEN IS AN ANIMAL TERMED A VERTEBRATE? 283

WHY DO ANIMALS BECOME EXTINCT? 284
WHY DO AMPHIBIANS LEAVE THE WATER? 285

WHEN ARE SEEDS FORMED? 286
WHEN DOES POLLINATION TAKE PLACE? 287

WHEN DO WATER-DWELLING INSECTS BREATHE? 288

WHEN DID THE FIRST PLANTS APPEAR?

Plants are organisms that use light as a source of energy and to produce the food they need in order to live and grow. The Earth's original atmosphere contained poisonous gases. The lack of oxygen meant that no animals or plants could survive on the Earth. The earliest plants or plant-like bacteria began the process of photosynthesis, which releases oxygen as well as a waste product. This gas gradually built up in the atmosphere as the plant life spread, making it possible for oxygen-dependent animals to evolve.

Coral was formed by bacteria in much the same way as plants. It is made up of a variety of invertebrate marine organisms of a stonelike, horny, or leathery consistency. They live in colonies begun by just one polyp. Each polyp builds a hard skeleton around itself.

Coral reef

FACT FILE

Lichens are a mixture of algae and fungi. Many grow like a mat over rocks or tree trunks, while others look like a small branched plant.

WHEN IS CLIMAX VEGETATION ACHIEVED?

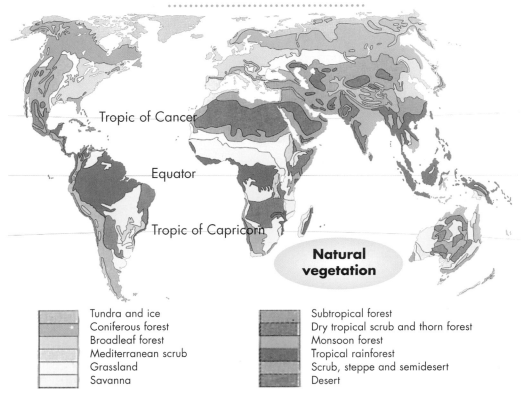

Tropic of Cancer

Equator

Tropic of Capricorn

Natural vegetation

Tundra and ice	
Coniferous forest	
Broadleaf forest	
Mediterranean scrub	
Grassland	
Savanna	

Subtropical forest	
Dry tropical scrub and thorn forest	
Monsoon forest	
Tropical rainforest	
Scrub, steppe and semidesert	
Desert	

When vegetation first starts growing in newly formed soil, it is at a disadvantage because the soil will not be nutrient-rich. As the plants die, they enrich the soil, allowing more plants to take advantage of this. As the soil gets older, it has gleaned more and more nutrients from dead plants – and more and more plants are able to grow successfully in the soil. Climax vegetation occurs when the vegetation is totally suited to the soil in the given climate. In reality, this can never last permanently due to the ever-changing environment.

FACT FILE

Rainforests have developed in areas where the soil is very fertile and where there is a great deal of rainfall. The varied vegetation suggests the soil is extremely nutrient-rich.

WHEN DID DARWIN SAIL TO THE GALAPAGOS ISLANDS?

The marine iguana

In the year 1831 Charles Darwin (1809–1882) set out on an exploratory voyage in the ship Beagle, heading for South America. The voyage lasted five years and during this time Darwin kept careful notes of everything he saw, in particular the strange animal life on the Galapagos Islands, off the western coast of Ecuador. He was disturbed by the fact that the birds and tortoises of the Galapagos Islands tended to resemble species found on the nearby continent, while inhabits of similar adjoining islands to the Galapagos had quite different animal populations. In London, Darwin later learned that the finches he had brought back belonged to a different species, not merely different varieties, as he had originally believed.

FACT FILE

When Charles Darwin first published his theories on evolution they created a sensation, but it took a while before they were accepted.

WHEN DID DARWIN PUBLISH *ON THE ORIGIN OF SPECIES?*

A Galapagos-dwelling tortoise

Upon his return from the voyage, Darwin turned over all the specimens he had brought back to cataloguing experts in Cambridge and London. In South America he had found fossils of extinct armadillos that were similar but not identical to the living animals he had seen. On November 24, 1859 Darwin published his theories in a book called *On the Origin of Species*. It caused a great sensation, but it was some time before it was accepted by the scientific world. The first edition sold out immediately and by 1872 the work had run through six editions. It became generally accepted that evolution took place along the lines that Darwin suggested. His theory on evolution of species solved many puzzles.

FACT FILE

We can see how evolution has changed living things by examining fossils. Fossils preserve the body parts of living creatures from long ago so that we can see how they have changed over millions of years.

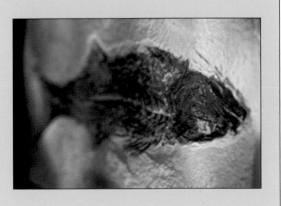

Carl Linnaeus

WHY DID LINNAEUS DEVELOP A CLASSIFICATION SYSTEM?

Carl Linnaeus (1707–1778) was a Swedish botanist and explorer who was the first to create a uniform system for naming plants and animals. Most plants and animals have popular names that vary from place to place. Scientific names are given so that the same name is recognized everywhere. Latin is the language used for scientific names. The scientific names are in two parts. The first is the generic name, which describes a group of related living things, and the second name is the specific name, which applies only to that living thing.

FACT FILE

The Latin name of the White Water Lily is *Nymphaea alba*. They are one of a group of plants whose flowers close up for the night.

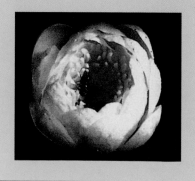

WHEN IS AN ANIMAL TERMED A VERTEBRATE?

An animal is classed as a vertebrate when it has a backbone to provide support for the muscles and protection for the spinal cord. Vertebrates include fish, amphibians, reptiles, birds and mammals. The backbone is actually a series of small bones called vertebrae. They are joined together and locked with rope-like ligaments to provide a flexible but extremely strong anchor for the back muscles. The spinal cord runs down a channel inside the vertebrae, providing protection from damage. Some primitive fish, such as sharks and rays, have a spine made of a tough rubbery material called cartilage. There are approximately 45,000 living species of vertebrates. In size, they range from minute fishes to elephants and whales (of up to 100 tons), the largest animals ever to have existed. They are adapted to life underground, on the surface, and in the air.

FACT FILE

The duck-billed platypus is a very unusual, small, semiaquatic mammal. It lives in lakes and streams of eastern Australia and Tasmania. It is notable in having a broad, flat, rubbery snout, webbed feet, and in that it lays eggs.

WHY DO ANIMALS BECOME EXTINCT?

GIANT PANDA: fewer than 1,000 remaining in the wild

YELLOW-EYED PENGUIN: about 3,000 left in the wild

RED WOLF: only 200 exist in captivity, none in the wild

According to the theory of evolution, some animal species become extinct because they are less successful than other species that gradually replace them.

These so-called 'failed' animals are also unable to adapt to changing circumstances. Humans have speeded up their extinction by changing the environment so rapidly that animals do not have the time to adapt. For example, the destruction of Indonesian rainforests has left nowhere for the orang-utan to live. It would take millions of years for the animal to evolve into a ground-living creature. Hunting is the main reason for the reduced numbers and probable extinction of animals such as the tiger, the blue whale, and the giant panda.

FACT FILE

The black rhino has been reduced to about 2,550 as a result of poaching. Most of the ones that survive today live in protected game parks.

WHY DO AMPHIBIANS LEAVE THE WATER?

Although frogs and toads can live on land, they have to return to the water to breed. Common frogs can be found in many freshwater habitats. They often show up in garden ponds, but are just as happy in lakes, canals and pools. Toads usually prefer wooded ponds and lakes and can sometimes be seen in boggy pools.

Frogs and toads are amphibians, which means they are equally at home on land and water. Toads, however, spend more time away from water than most frogs. Their skin is leathery and warty and they do not lose water so easily on dry land. On land, a frog hops to escape danger, whereas a toad will walk. The bodies of some frogs and toads have adapted to survive in very dry conditions, such as in deserts.

FACT FILE

A frog's eyes are on top of its head so it can see above the water's surface. This way it can keep a watch out for predators.

WHEN ARE SEEDS FORMED?

Seeds are the main means by which flowering plants reproduce and spread. After the plant has been fertilized the egg cells develop into a seed from which a new plant can develop. The seed contains an embryo from which the new plant will grow. It also contains a food store to nourish the embryo until it has developed roots and leaves. The seed is enclosed in a tough outer coating to protect it from drying out. Many seeds can be carried by the wind. Some even have a fluffy umbrella like the dandelion seed head (above), which enables them to be carried for very long distances.

FACT FILE

The biggest seed is the coco de mer, a kind of coconut that grows in the Seychelles, a group of islands in the Indian Ocean. The coco de mer seeds weigh 20 kg (44 lbs) each.

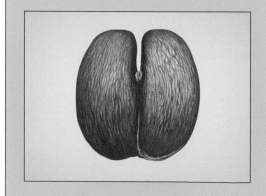

WHEN DOES POLLINATION TAKE PLACE?

TELL ME ABOUT SCIENCE & TECHNOLOGY : THE NATURAL WORLD

FACT FILE

The flowers of orchids are highly specialized for pollination by insects. When the insect pushes into the flower to reach the nectar, the pollinia stick onto its head.

Pollination is the process of transferring pollen from the stamen to stigma. It is possible for flowers to pollinate themselves, or other flowers on the same plant – this is called self-pollination. It is, however, much better for the health of the species if cross-pollination occurs, i.e. pollen is transferred from one plant to another. The most common method involves insects that are attracted to the flowers for their nectar. Pollen grains stick to the insects' bodies and are effectively transferred from one plant to another as the insect moves from flower to flower. Other, less attractive types of flower, use wind to transport their pollen.

WHEN DO WATER-DWELLING INSECTS BREATHE?

The saucer bug

Water bugs are found in all sorts of different types of freshwater habitats. They all breathe air and have to return to the surface of the water from time to time. Ponds and lakes are the best habitats for water bugs. Only a few species live in streams and rivers, except where the current is slow-flowing. Adult water beetles have to breathe air. They do

not have gills. Many have a supply of air beneath their wing cases or under the body, which they renew from time to time. Watch a beetle in a tank. Some species come to the surface tail-first, while a few come to the surface head first. Count the number of times a beetle will visit the surface in an hour.

Adult water beetle

FACT FILE

Place a needle on a piece of paper in some water. As the paper sinks, the needle floats, showing surface tension. This same process allows the water boatman to 'walk' on water. It uses its legs like oars to swim.

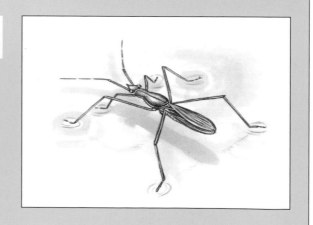

Discoveries & Inventions

HOW DOES A BATTERY PRODUCE ELECTRICITY? 290
HOW DOES AN ELECTRIC LIGHT WORK? 291

HOW DO LASERS WORK? 292
HOW DO AEROPLANES FLY? 293

HOW DOES SONAR WORK? 294
HOW DO BATS USE SONAR? 295

WHEN WAS PAPER FIRST MADE? 296
WHEN WERE THE FIRST BOOKS MADE? 297

WHEN WERE FIREWORKS INTRODUCED? 298
WHEN WAS GUNPOWDER FIRST USED? 299

WHO FIRST SPLIT THE ATOM? 300
WHEN WAS ATOMIC STRUCTURE DISCOVERED? 301

WHY ARE MICROSCOPES USED? 302

HOW DOES A BATTERY PRODUCE ELECTRICITY?

The electric current we use for power can be produced in two ways, by big machines known as dynamos and generators, and by the portable method of battery cells. Electricity is produced by the the battery cell by changing chemical energy into electrical energy, with some of the chemical energy being converted into heat and the rest into electric current. A battery contains two different conductors, or electrodes. The electrodes are separated by a conducting liquid or paste, called the electrolyte. The substances in the battery react chemically with each other to produce an electrical current. As a result of chemical activity, a positive charge builds up at one electrode and this can flow through a conductor such as a wire to the other (negative) electrode.

FACT FILE

An alternative form of power has arrived with the development of wind farms. Huge windmills situated on exposed and windy areas drive dynamos to produce electricity.

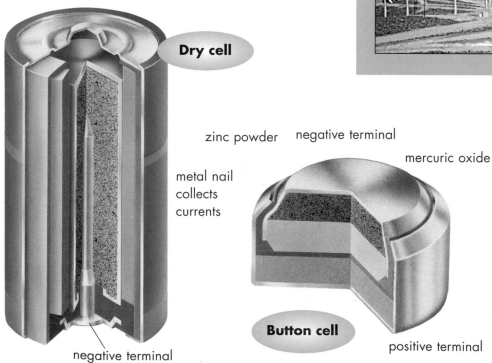

positive terminal

Dry cell

zinc powder

negative terminal

mercuric oxide

metal nail collects currents

Button cell

negative terminal

positive terminal

HOW DOES AN ELECTRIC LIGHT WORK?

sealed glass bulb

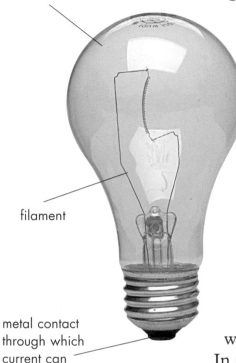

filament

metal contact through which current can flow

Some of the earliest experiments that led to the electric light bulb were conducted by an English scientist, Humphrey Davey. Using a very weak version of what we would now call a battery, he first connected wires to its ends and then attached a piece of carbon to the other ends of the wires. Davey found he could produce a sparking light by touching the two pieces of carbon together and then drawing them slightly apart.

Called 'an electric arc', it was the first real evidence that light produced by electricity was possible, although the source of the power in these early bulbs was certainly not strong enough.

In a modern light bulb a current is passed through a very thin filament of metal that has a high resistance to the flow of electricity. The filament becomes white-hot and produces light. The bulb contains an inert gas so the filament will not burn.

FACT FILE

Lightning is actually electricity. A huge electrical charge can be built up in certain weather conditions, and this leads to thunderstorms when a bolt of lightning leaps between the earth and a cloud. The air is heated to a tremendous temperature, causing the explosive noise of thunder as it suddenly expands.

HOW DO LASERS WORK?

Lasers are devices that produce a narrow beam of extremely strong light. Lasers amplify light by causing photons to be bounced back and forth in a substance (which can be solid, liquid or gas), which add extra energy. The result is that intense light is emitted in a very narrow beam. The intense beam of light produced by a laser can be used to produce images for publicity or entertainment purposes.

Lasers are also used to cut metal, and for precision cuts in operations. In CD players, laser light is scanned across the CD's silvery surface, reading the tiny changes in light reflected back. They are also used in office printers and scanners. In engineering, the intense narrow beam of light is used to measure and align roads and tunnels.

FACT FILE

Lasers are used everyday in our shops and banks to scan banknotes to see whether they are forgeries. This is done by passing the note under an ultraviolet light scanner.

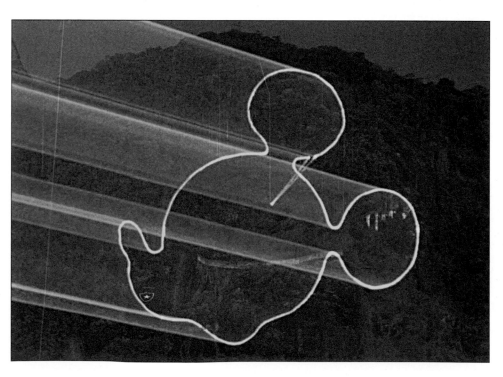

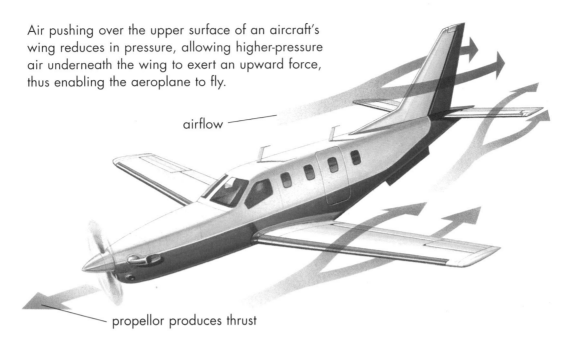

Air pushing over the upper surface of an aircraft's wing reduces in pressure, allowing higher-pressure air underneath the wing to exert an upward force, thus enabling the aeroplane to fly.

airflow

propellor produces thrust

HOW DO AEROPLANES FLY?

As an aeroplane moves through the air, the air passes over the surface of its wings. These wings are shaped with a curved top surface and a flatter lower surface, which means that air passing over the top of the wing has to travel a little faster than that below the wing. This causes the pressure to lower above the wing, while the air pressure below pushes up. The end result is the lift that keeps the aeroplane in the air.

The tail surfaces of the aeroplane keep the wing at the proper angle to provide the right amount of lift. The power to propel the aeroplane along can come either from the engine, or, in the case of gliders, from rising air currents.

Jet engines propel a plane just like a rocket, with a stream of hot gases.

FACT FILE

Leonardo da Vinci (1452–1519) drew his plans for a helicopter hundreds of years before flying machines were even invented.

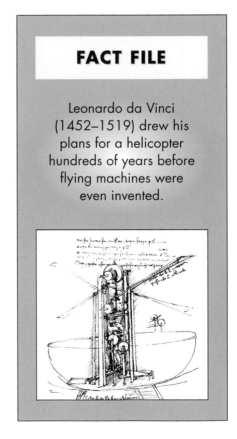

HOW DOES SONAR WORK?

Sound waves travel extremely well through water. They are used to detect submarines, wrecks on the seabed, or by fishermen to find shoals of fish. A sonar device under a ship sends out sound waves that travel down through the water. The sound waves are reflected back from any solid object they reach, such as shoals of fish or the seabed.

The echoes are received by the ship and can be used to 'draw' an image of the object, and its location, onto a computer screen.

FACT FILE

Supersonic aircraft actually break the sound barrier. When travelling at such very high speeds, aircraft begin to build up a huge wave of compressed air in front of them causing a sonic 'boom'.

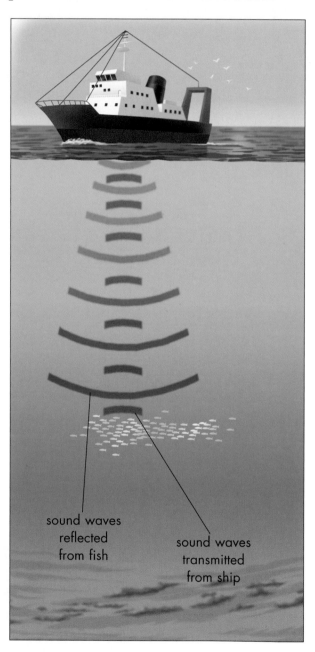

sound waves reflected from fish

sound waves transmitted from ship

Sonar, or echo sounding is used by fishermen to detect shoals of fish. It can also be used to detect submarines or to find wrecks on the seabed.

HOW DO BATS USE SONAR?

Bats also use sonar waves to navigate. Bats are nocturnal, which means they are active at night and sleep during the day. Since bats have to hunt for their food at night, you would imagine that they need exceptionally good eyesight. But this is not the case, as bats do not depend on their eyes for getting about. When bats fly, they utter a series of very high pitched sounds, which are too high to be heard by the human ear.

The echoes from these sounds are thrown back to the bat when it is in flight, and it can tell whether the echo came from an obstacle nearby or far away. The bat can then change its course in flight to avoid hitting the obstacle!

Bats produce a continuous high-pitched squeaking in flight, and the echoes from this sound allow them to navigate in darkness and even to locate the small flying insects on which they feed.

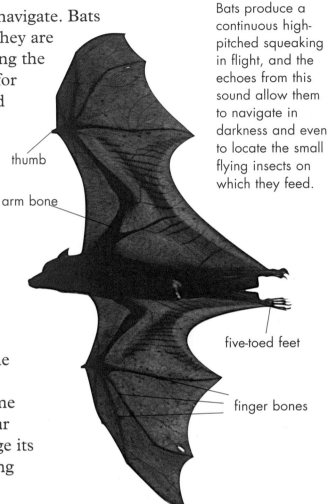

thumb

arm bone

five-toed feet

finger bones

FACT FILE

Musical instruments produce sounds in various different ways, but they all cause air to vibrate to carry the sound to your ears. Sounds travel as waves and it is the shape of the sound wave that determines the kind of sound that will be produced. The pitch of the sound (whether high or low) depends on the frequency of the sound waves.

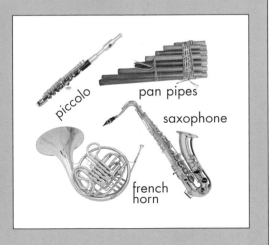

piccolo

pan pipes

saxophone

french horn

WHEN WAS PAPER FIRST MADE?

The first paper was made about 2,000 years ago in China, by a man called Ts'ai Lun. He took the stringy inner bark of the Mulberry tree and pounded it in water until it became a mass of flattened threads. He then placed this pulped solution onto a flat tray of fine bamboo strips.

The water was allowed to drain through the bamboo, and the threads in the bamboo were left to dry. The dried result was a flat, fibrous material considered to be the very first paper. As with all new discoveries, improvements are gradually made.

One of these was to brush starch over the paper to improve it.

The secret of papermaking soon became world-wide knowledge as Chinese traders travelled to Russia and the Middle East. From there, the art of papermaking spread to Europe.

A revolutionary invention, paper-making began to be produced in mass quantities. The first continuous paper-making machine was developed in France in 1798 by Louis Robert. At the beginning of the next century, the Fourdrinier brothers in London developed the idea further.

FACT FILE

The Chinese had another secret, they were the only people who knew how to make silk. European traders would make the long journey to take silk back to Europe.

WHEN WERE THE FIRST BOOKS MADE?

The Diamond Sutta, the oldest printed book known, made in 868 AD

The first books were made about 4,000 years ago by the Egyptians who took flattened layers of papyrus stems to make sheets. The 'books' they made were collections of rolled papyrus sheets – very different to a book of today.

In the middle of the fifth century, parchment (sheep skin) replaced papyrus. Parchment sheets were placed on top of one another and bound down one side with leather tongs.

But it was in the Middle Ages that books as we know them today evolved. Vellum (calf skin) was made into sheets, and each piece was folded down the middle. Four vellum sheets made eight leaves and was considered a section. Unlike parchment, vellum was thick enough to be written on both sides. Finished sections were sewn together down the back fold (the spine) and covered with wooden boards front and back. The boards and spine were then covered with leather; the result was a book similar to that of today.

FACT FILE

In about 500 AD monks would spend endless hours on illuminated handwritten books. The work was slow and painstaking, but worthwhile because it was another way to show dedication to God.

WHEN WERE FIREWORKS INTRODUCED?

Chinese crackers were probably the first fireworks to be made and this was about 2000 years ago. They are still used in China and throughout the East to celebrate weddings, births and religious festivals. They are also used to scare away evil spirits. It is probable that gunpowder was developed in China because they used potassium nitrate (saltpetre) to cure their meat, and so it was readily available.

Fireworks have also been used for centuries in ancient Indian and Siamese ceremonies. The earliest recorded use of gunpowder in England is by the Franciscan monk Roger Bacon (born 1214). He recorded his experiments with a mixture which was very inadequate by today's standards but was recognisable as gunpowder. His formula contained charcoal and sulphur because there was no natural source of saltpeter available.

FACT FILE

In January 1606 Parliament established November 5 as a day of public thanksgiving. The day, known as Guy Fawkes Day, is still celebrated with bonfires, fireworks, and the carrying of 'guys' through the streets.

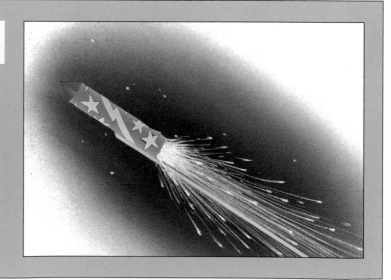

WHEN WAS GUNPOWDER FIRST USED?

It was the Chinese again who first started using gunpowder in warfare. By the year 1232, the Chinese had discovered black powder (gunpowder) and had learned to use it to make explosive bombs as well as propelling forces for rockets. Drawings made in military documents later show powder rockets tied to arrows and spears.

When the Mongols laid siege to the city of K'ai-feng, the capital of Honan province, the Chinese defenders used weapons that were described as 'arrows of flying fire'. In the same battle, it is reported, the defenders dropped from the walls of the city a kind of bomb described as 'heaven-shaking thunder'.

In the same century, rockets appeared in Europe. There is indication that their first use was by the Mongols in the Battle of Legnica in 1241. The Arabs are also reported to have used rockets in 1249.

FACT FILE

Guy Fawkes is best known for his efforts to blow up the Parliament building in 1605. This became known as the 'Gunpowder Plot'. His plan, however, was foiled and he was consequently arrested on 4 November, 1605.

WHO FIRST SPLIT THE ATOM?

Ernest Rutherford (1871–1937) was a physicist who studied radioactivity. He found several different forms of radiation and also discovered that elements change as a result of radioactive decay. He received the Nobel Prize for his work. Rutherford went on to discover the nucleus of the atom, and in 1919 he finally succeeded in splitting an atom for the first time.

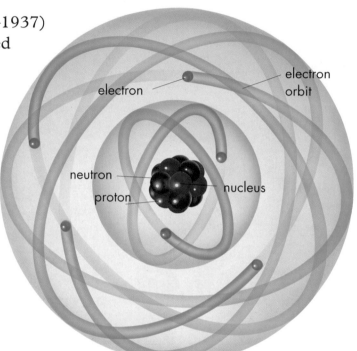

He described the atom as a tiny, dense, positively charged core called a nucleus, in which nearly all the mass is concentrated, around which the light, negative constituents, called electrons, circulate at some distance, much like planets revolving around the Sun.

FACT FILE

Atoms become linked to other atoms by electrical bonds, which work rather like chemical hooks. Some atoms only carry one of these hooks while others may have many.

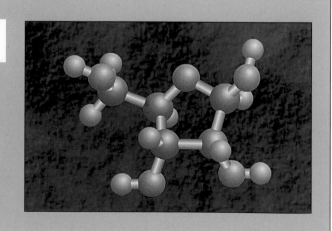

WHEN WAS ATOMIC STRUCTURE DISCOVERED?

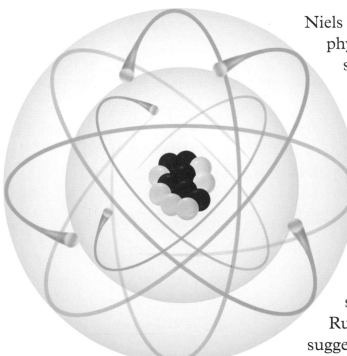

Niels Bohr was a Danish physicist. His mark on science and history was worldwide. His professional work and personal convictions were part of the larger stories of the century. Bohr studied physics at the University of Copenhagen where he began to work on the problem of the atom's structure. Ernest Rutherford had recently suggested the atom had a miniature, dense nucleus surrounded by a cloud of nearly weightless electrons. There were a few problems with the model, however. Bohr proposed adding to the model, and this proved to be a huge leap forward in making theory fit the experimental evidence that other physicists had brought to light. A few inaccuracies remained to be ironed out by others over the next few years, but his essential idea was proved correct.

He received the Nobel Prize for this work in 1922, and it is what he is most famous for. He was only 37 at the time, and went on to make many other discoveries.

FACT FILE

Niels Bohr helped to develop the atomic bomb in 1943.

WHY ARE MICROSCOPES USED?

The microscope enables us to see minute things which are otherwise invisible to the naked eye. Its name comes from the Greek 'mikros' for 'small' and skopos for 'watcher', the instrument being a 'watcher of small things'.

Things appear bigger as we bring them closer to the eye, yet when they get too close, anything less than 10 inches (25.5cm), they become blurred or out of focus. But the object can be brought nearer, and still stay in focus, with the aid of a simple convex lens that is placed between the eye and the object.

It was a Dutchman called Antonie van Leeuwenhoek (1632–1723) who discovered ground glass lenses, which he used to examine the world about him. In the 1670s he made his first crude microscope with a tiny lens. This allowed him to be the first person to see microscopic life such as bacteria, yeast and living blood cells. From his pioneering work came an instrument which is now used in every branch of science and industry.

FACT FILE

Some microscopes are so powerful they can magnify the smallest objects many thousands of times. This plant cell would be invisible to the human eye without the use of magnification.

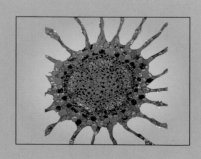

The Solar System

WHAT IS THE MOON? 304
WHAT IS THE MOON MADE OF? 305

WHY DOES THE EARTH TRAVEL AROUND THE SUN? 306
WHAT IS THE SUN MADE OF? 307

WHAT IS THE MILKY WAY? 308
WHAT IS A STAR? 309

WHAT IS A SUPERNOVA? 310
WHAT IS A NEBULA? 311

WHAT ARE THE PLANETS OF THE SOLAR SYSTEM? 312
WHAT ARE THE RINGS OF SATURN? 313

WHAT WAS THE BIG BANG? 314
WHAT IS THE UNIVERSE MADE UP OF? 315

WHY IS NEPTUNE BLUE? 316
WHAT DOES VENUS LOOK LIKE? 317

WHAT ARE THE MAGELLANIC CLOUDS? 318
WHAT IS THE SOLAR WIND? 319

WHAT IS A BLACK HOLE? 320

WHAT IS THE MOON?

The Moon is the Earth's only satellite, and it has been orbiting our planet for at least 4,000 million years. It is a rocky sphere about 2,160 miles (3,476 km) in diameter, which is about one-quarter the size of the Earth.

Scientists believe that the Moon formed when another planet about the size of Mars collided with the Earth. The collision splashed a huge mass of molten (liquid) rock into space. This molten rock quickly formed into a sphere, and the Moon cooled into its solid form. The Moon's surface is heavily pitted by collisions with debris such as asteroids.

FACT FILE

Living things need air and water to stay alive, and neither of these is available on the Moon. The Moon also suffers extreme temperature swings between the lunar day and night.

WHAT IS THE MOON MADE OF?

The Moon is a rocky satellite, and is made of similar material to the Earth. It has an outer layer, or mantle, of rock, and a core that is probably made up mostly of iron. Unlike the Earth's liquid mantle, the interior of the Moon is cool and solid. There is little or no volcanic activity on the Moon. However, while it was cooling, early in its life, floods and streams of lava ran out across the Moon's surface. The Moon also has mountain ranges, many of which are the remains of impact craters and volcanoes that were active when the Moon was still hot. There are some huge valleys called rilles, which can be hundreds of miles in length and look a little like river-beds.

FACT FILE

The first man on the Moon was Neil Armstrong, accompanied by Buzz Aldrin, on 20th July 1969. They travelled to the Moon on Apollo 11.

WHY DOES THE EARTH TRAVEL AROUND THE SUN?

One theory explaining the origin of our solar system is that a huge dust cloud was formed about 5 billion years ago. Spinning through space, it gradually flattened out into a disc shape, the hot centre forming the Sun. At the same time, the outer portions of the dust cloud spun off into space, breaking away from the centre in swirling masses to become the planets. The reason these planets, including the Earth, didn't just fly off into space, was the gravitational pull of the Sun.

It is this force that keeps the Earth revolving round the Sun in what we call its 'orbit'. The speed a planet moves in its orbit depends on its distance from the Sun. When closer it moves faster. The Earth moves at 18.8 miles (30 km) per second when closest to the Sun, and 18.2 miles (29 km) per second at its furthest point away.

FACT FILE

Other planets that revolve around the Sun are Mercury and Pluto. Mercury is the closest planet to the Sun and moves at an average speed of 29.8 miles (48 km) per second.

WHAT IS THE SUN MADE OF?

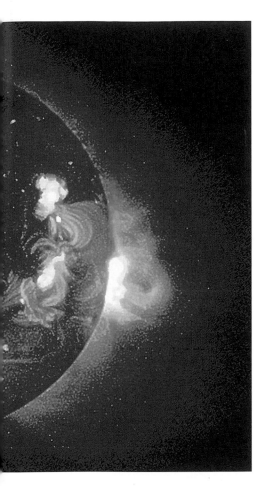

The Sun is a great ball of hot gases, made up of many layers. Astronomers have obtained many of their facts about the Sun by using special instruments. These instruments enable the scientists to study the glowing gases of the Sun and to see how different substances are distributed on the Sun and to take photographs of the Sun's corona without causing damage to the eyes. Finally, these instruments study radio waves that are emitted by the Sun. Because the Earth's atmosphere stops many of the Sun's radiations from reaching the Earth, scientists send instruments high up into the atmosphere. Such space probes help them learn more about the Sun.

FACT FILE

Without the Sun, life would be impossible on Earth. Among other things, the atmosphere would be frozen, no green plants would be living, and there would be no rain.

WHAT IS THE MILKY WAY?

One of the most spectacular features of the night sky that has fascinated men since ancient times is the Milky Way, which stretches from one horizon to the other. Many years ago, people imagined it was a pathway for the angels to travel to heaven, but today we know the truth about it, which is just as remarkable.

If it could be looked down upon from above, our galaxy would appear as a huge disc, round and flat like an enormous watch. But our vantage point, as part of the galaxy, is from within the 'watch' looking out towrds its edge. So it's that edge that we see, curving around us with its millions of stars twinkling in it, as the Milky Way.

FACT FILE

Containing at least 3,000,000,000 stars, the galaxy is so big we can hardly imagine its size. While the light from the Sun takes eight minutes to reach the Earth, the light from the middle of the galaxy takes about 27,000 years to reach the Sun.

WHAT IS A STAR?

Stars are huge balls of burning gas that are scattered throughout the Universe. They burn for millions of years, giving off both light and heat. Stars produce energy by a process called nuclear fusion. The coolest stars are red and dim, while the hottest stars give off blue-white light. The temperatures on their surface range from 3,500°C for cooler stars to over 40,000°C for the hottest stars.

A new star is born when gas and dust are drawn together by gravity, forming a huge clump. It heats up until nuclear fusion begins, and the new star appears in the sky.

FACT FILE

Stars die when they eventually use up all their fuel and burn out, but this process takes many millions of years. Towards the end of its life, a star starts to run out of hydrogen to power its nuclear fusion. It starts to cool, becoming a red giant.

WHAT IS A SUPERNOVA?

Sometimes a star appears in the sky quite suddenly. This happens when there are a pair of stars rotating together. These are called binaries, and there is usually one large star called a red giant, orbiting with a smaller, hotter star. The nova takes place when gas is drawn from the red giant into the smaller star, where the heat causes a massive explosion and emits huge amounts of light. A supernova takes place when a star collapses as it begins to burn out, then suddenly explodes, producing a huge amount of light energy, and leaving behind a tiny core of neutrons, which is the heaviest substance in the Universe.

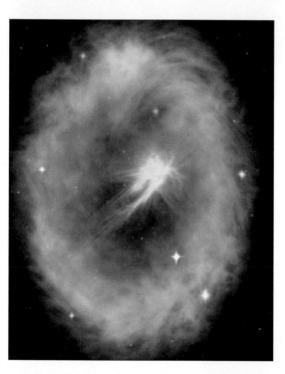

FACT FILE

Even with today's most powerful and advanced equipment, there is no visible limit to the Universe. No one is totally sure of the shape of the Universe.

WHAT IS A NEBULA?

FACT FILE

The only diffuse nebula visible to the naked eye is the beautiful Orion Nebula.

A nebula is a huge cloud of white-hot gas and solid material that whirls about in interstellar space getting smaller and hotter all the time. As the gas cloud grows smaller, it throws off rings of gas. Each of these rings condenses to become a star. Based on appearance, nebulae can be divided into two broad classes: dark nebulae and bright nebulae. Dark nebulae appear as irregularly shaped black patches in the sky and blot out the light of the stars lying beyond them. Bright nebulae appear as faintly luminous, glowing surfaces; they either emit their own light or reflect the light of nearby stars.

311

WHAT ARE THE PLANETS OF THE SOLAR SYSTEM?

The four planets that are nearest to the Sun are called the inner planets. In order from the Sun, they are Mercury, Venus, Earth and Mars. The inner planets are different from the outer planets, which are farther away from the Sun, because they are made of rock. Each of the inner planets has an atmosphere. However, apart from the Earth, the atmospheres of the inner planets are very thin and would be poisonous to humans. The outer planets, which are Jupiter, Saturn, Uranus, Neptune and Pluto are composed mostly of frozen gases, so although they are very large, they are comparatively light.

FACT FILE

Science fiction writers thought that life might exist beneath the thick clouds of Venus. We now know that conditions there are too extreme for life as we know it.

WHAT ARE THE RINGS OF SATURN?

Shining rings of billions of tiny chips of ice, rock and dust surround Saturn. The rings reflect light strongly and can be clearly seen through a telescope from the Earth. It was first thought that Saturn had three wide rings, but it is now known that the rings are actually made up of thousands of narrow ringlets. The rings are only 328 ft (100 m) thick, but extend into space for 47,000 miles (76,000 km). The material in the rings was probably captured by Saturn's gravity when the Solar System was forming, or it might be the remains of a moon that has broken up. Space probes recently discovered that some of the rings are braided, or twisted.

WHAT WAS THE BIG BANG?

Nobody knows how the Universe began, but the most common theory is the Big Bang. According to this theory, the Universe was formed from an immense explosion 13 billion years ago. Before the Big Bang, everything in the Universe was packed into a tiny area, smaller than the nucleus of an atom. This point was called a singularity and was incredibly hot. It was released in an explosion so powerful that all of the matter in the singularity was blasted into an area larger than a galaxy in less than a fraction of a second. There is very strong evidence to support the theory of the Big Bang. The strongest 'proof' is a weak signal that has been detected in space. This is thought to be an echo from the energy released by the force of the Big Bang.

FACT FILE

According to ancient Egyptian mythology, the fundamentals of life – air (Shu) and moisture (Tefnut) – came from the spittle of their Sun God Re. From the union of Shu and Tefnut came Geb, the Earth god, and Nut, the sky goddess. The first human beings were born from Re's tears.

WHAT IS THE UNIVERSE MADE UP OF?

The Universe is everything and anything that exists. The Universe is still a mystery to scientists. It is made up almost entirely of hydrogen and helium. These are the two lightest elements. All the rest of the matter in the Universe is very rare. Elements such as silicon, carbon and others are concentrated into clouds, stars and planets. The Universe is held together by four invisible forces. Gravity and electromagnetism are the two familiar forces. The other two kinds are strong and weak nuclear forces. These operate only inside the incredibly tiny nuclei of atoms, holding the tiny particles together.

FACT FILE

Nobody knows exactly how big the Universe is, what shape it takes, where it comes from or what it is expanding into. If we could go far enough into space, maybe we could understand more.

WHY IS NEPTUNE BLUE?

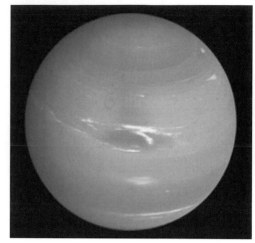

Neptune is covered with a blue ocean of liquid methane. It is a very cold place – at the farthest part of its orbit it is 4,000 million km from the Sun. Its surface temperature drops to –210°C. Neptune is made of hydrogen, helium, and methane, and probably has a rocky core. It takes an amazing 164.8 years to travel just once around the Sun. Neptune was first identified in 1846 when astronomers found that an unidentified planet was disturbing the orbit of Uranus. Neptune has huge storms and one of these, the Great Dark Spot, was larger than the Earth.

FACT FILE

Mars is covered by a stony desert that contains lots of iron oxide, making it appear rusty-red. Mars has small polar ice-caps that grow larger during the Martian winter.

WHAT DOES VENUS LOOK LIKE?

Venus is often referred to as Earth's sister. The planet is a similar size to our own, but here the resemblance ends. The temperature on the surface of the planet is nearly 500°C (930°F). The air is dense enough to crush a human in seconds, and the atmosphere consists partly of acid. The dark patches that you see on the surface of Venus are a layer of cloud 19 miles (30 km) thick. If we look past the clouds, we can see that Venus is a planet once ruled by volcanoes. Scientists believe that there are at least 160 that are larger than 62 miles (100 km) in diameter and over 50,000 smaller ones. However, there is no evidence to show that these volcanoes are still active today.

FACT FILE

Because Venus was the Roman goddess of love, astronomers have named many of the planet's features after famous women.

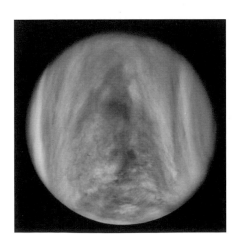

WHAT ARE THE MAGELLANIC CLOUDS?

The two galaxies which are closest to our own galaxy the Milky Way, the Magellanic Clouds, are visible as faint areas of light in the night sky of the Southern Hemishere. Because the arrangement of stars within them does not follow a regular pattern, they are classified by astronomers as irregular galaxies.

They appear cloudy to the naked eye because although they include billions of stars, individual stars in these galaxies can only be seen with

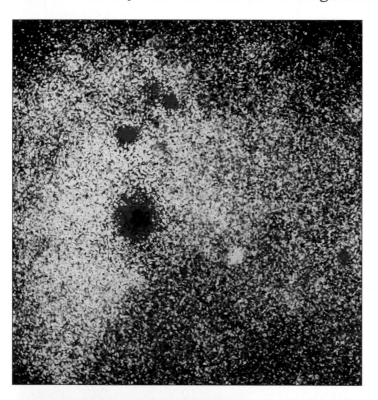

the use of the most powerful telescopes.

The Magellanic Clouds also consist of an enormous quantity of gas, which is mostly composed of hydrogen, from which new stars are continually being formed. Also, much of the light that does emanate from the Magellanic Clouds originates from the young, hot blue stars that are surrounded by almost luminous clouds of this gas.

FACT FILE

Magellanic Clouds were first recorded in the early 1500s during the circumglobal voyage of the Portuguese explorer Ferdinand Magellan, after whom they were named.

WHAT IS THE SOLAR WIND?

Charged particles are constantly being given off by the Sun. They are known as the Solar Wind and are strongest when the sunspot activity is at its height. When the Solar Wind reaches the Earth's magnetic field, the charged particles interact with gases in the Earth's atmosphere 6 miles (10 km) above the surface. This interaction causes the particles to send out light, which is seen from Earth as an amazing lightshow, most visible within the polar circles. In the Northern Hemisphere this is known as the aurora borealis, and in the Southern Hemisphere as the aurora australis.

FACT FILE

Darker areas on the surface of the Sun are called sunspots. These areas of cooler gas occur when the Sun's magnetic field blocks the flow of heat from the core.

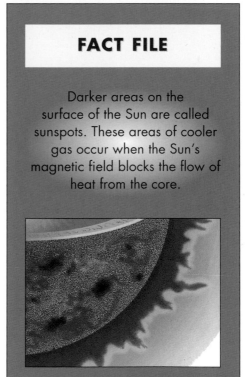